D0249169

Academic Bonding and Social Concern

The Society of Christian Ethics
1959-1983

Academic Bonding and Social Concern

The Society of Christian Ethics 1959-1983

Edward LeRoy Long, Jr.

Published by Religious Ethics, Incorporated

Copyright © 1984 by
Edward LeRoy Long, Jr.

Library of Congress Cataloging in Publication Data

Long, Edward LeRoy.
Academic bonding and social concern.

1. Society of Christian Ethics (U.S.)–History.
2. Social Ethics. I. Title.
BJ1188.7.S633L66 1985 241'.006'073 84-24935
ISBN 0-268-00614-8 (pbk.)

Manufactured in the United States of America

Contents

Preface

The Society of Christian Ethics is a scholarly association that has played a uniquely meaningful role in the lives of its members. In some respects it has maintained remarkable continuities in its life since it sprang into being in 1959 from a parent group called The American Society of Seminary Professors of Christian Social Ethics in the United States and Canada. It has also undergone significant transformations. This history, which was commissioned in connection with the twenty-fifth anniversary of the Society, attempts to present as accurately as possible the details of the Society's life and to reflect on that life as an experience of community.

Not many societies take themselves seriously enough to begin collecting historical records about their activities from the first days of their life. The Society of Christian Ethics is no exception. This means that records are spotty and, in many instances, non-existent. Surprisingly, there is a much fuller account of the first year of the Society's life than of some of the subsequent early years. There are very few records of the parent group. Until five years ago there was no deliberate attempt systematically to collect the records of the Society and its activities, though random materials of various sorts (often in multiple copies) were deposited by former executive secretaries, and others, in the George Arendts Research Library at Syracuse University. In preparing a preliminary version of this history for oral delivery at the twentieth anniversary of the Society I consulted the materials at Syracuse and then found that I had personal files equally voluminous and more extensive about some matters than those to be found there. I had kept things--for reasons I never consciously articulated at the time--like a pack rat. I have been able to share duplicates of them with the Arendts Library even as it has, with the permission of the Society's Executive Board, furnished me with copies of the materials which it holds.

In writing this version of the history for publication I

have been given materials by past executive secretaries as well as by other members of the Society. After arranging those and making an inventory, I then twice conducted canvasses for missing items. The first such canvass was a general request, detailing all needed items on one mimeographed sheet that was sent out in the late spring of 1979 as a special insert in the Society's general mailing calling for papers for the forthcoming 1980 program. That effort yielded only minimal returns. In January of 1983, after bringing the index of all items up-to-date, I wrote directly to those members from whom one or more items had not been forthcoming. That produced a much more satisfactory response. (Any good development professional could have told me that only the second approach would work, but alas some of us learn only by making our own mistakes.) These two efforts boosted the holdings in the archives to over three quarters of the papers given before the Society between 1959 and 1983. In time these will be placed in the George Arendts Research Library and probably in another convenient location so that future scholars can winnow them for even more insights than has been possible in this account.

In seeking to secure missing items it did not seem appropriate to badger those who had spoken as dignitaries or as guests of the Society for their contributions years after the fact. Many of them had spoken from notes and could not have reconstructed what they said. In other cases, such as workshops and panels, it did not prove promising to try to reconstruct the presentations, many of which were also given from notes. With these exceptions an effort was made to have the resulting record relatively as full as possible. It is complete as respects the printed programs of the annual meetings and the annual budgets. It is almost complete as respects minutes of the board meetings and the annual business meetings. There is a fairly good collection of the membership rosters from year-to-year. In the case of some annual meetings we have programs on which handwritten entries indicate last-minute changes occasioned by illness, weather, or the failure of certain persons to fulfill their commitments, and in such cases an effort has been made to report the happenings as they actually took place rather than as they were originally planned.

It is, of course, the ideal of every scholar to work with the highest possible accuracy. As one not trained or accustomed to writing primary history, doing this project has made me acutely aware of the enormous difficulties involved in such an undertaking. A historian of another professional group, whose account covered a much longer time span than does this one, once said in my hearing "Never again!" While not quite as emphatic about it, I certainly share the feeling behind the remark, and would urge any group that wants its history written at some future time to be very deliberate about collecting its records as they are produced--and, if possible, to have an archivist/historian responsible for collecting such data and reflecting on the life of the group on a continuing basis rather than asking someone to reconstruct the story after the events are forgotten or the records have been scattered.

The story as it is found in the materials which have thus been collected is made available here in a composite account which is being distributed to each and every member as economically as possible. It is with some fear and trepidation that this is sent forth, since I know that there are errors of detail that even the most careful attention has not been able to avoid. Just as the Roman Catholic church is wise in not canonizing saints until sometime after their death, perhaps prudent historians (which seem not to have the same license as journalists) do not write about others while they are still alive. I know from correspondence which has been done in connection with the project that people do not recall things with unfailing accuracy, even when they were directly involved. On some matters I have had to let documentary evidence override casual recollections. But to the extent errors remain I trust that there are none which will in any substantive way harm or damage individuals even if they do prove to be somewhat misleading or incidentally annoying.

This account covers a relatively short, and recent, period of time. It does not constitute a full account of the teaching of Christian ethics (or moral theology) during the period, nor is it intended to be an intellectual history of an academic discipline or disciplines. Rather, it is a record of the activities of a particular society during the first quarter-century of its officially constituted existence. The growth of this Society and the matters to which it gave attention in its programs does tell us something quite useful about the development of Christian ethics and/or Christian social ethics as subject matter fields and as a focus for professional engagement. While the story told here has obvious "in house" interest, much can be learned from it. It is to the credit of the officers and members of the Society that they saw the value of having such an account produced while the greater part of the necessary materials could be collected.

It is impossible to name individually all those who have given help in this undertaking. The roster of the Society itself should head the list, since without the response from those members who have been solicited for materials, asked to recall or verify special happenings, voluntarily sent information or suggestions, voted for budget items to support the expenses of the research, and finally paid the additional assessment making publication possible, this study could never have been completed. My gratitude to each and to all of these colleagues is not diminished even though they are not listed by name.

I would acknowledge specific help given by Max Stackhouse and Joseph Allen in reading large parts of the draft at different stages. Both caught errors of detail and perception. Thomas Ogletree was instrumental in supporting me in this undertaking--both as president of the Society during the year when most of the writing was done and as dean of the school that allowed me to use a good part of a sabbatical for this project.

The word processing department of Drew University has helped enormously in the preparation of the finished product. It worked with me to move both from rough copy to good copy and from good copy to camera-ready copy. This work was underwritten by the University, through the funds designated for scholarly productivity of the Theological School Faculty. I thank Mary Stringham in particular for her seemingly inexhaustible patience and skill in using a highly complicated machine acquired just prior to beginning work on this project. I appreciate help in copy editing given by Ellen Chmiel, a graduate student in Religion and Society at Drew. My wife, Grace Cumming Long, assisted in numerous ways. The Society is indebted to the *Journal of Religious Ethics*, and its editor, James Turner Johnson, for agreeing to publish this history.

E.L.L., Jr.

Drew Forest
Summer 1984

Part One
Beginnings

1

Background, Founding, and Early Years

The American Society of Christian Social Ethics in the United States and Canada, which through two subsequent name changes has become the present Society of Christian Ethics, was founded at a meeting in Washington, D.C., January 30-31, 1959. That meeting is taken as the official birthday of the Society, the twenty-fifth anniversary of which was celebrated at the annual meeting in Philadelphia, January 20-22, 1984.

There were several years of professional interaction among seminary professors of ethics and social ethics before 1959. Indeed, the 1959 meeting at Wesley Theological Seminary was as much the last meeting of an old group as it was the first meeting of a new organization. While the purposes and programs of the old group were remarkably similar to those that were to be characteristic of the new group, its organizational qualities were different. In a letter dated June 6, 1983, Paul Elman has written ". . . in the early days, the Society seemed less an organized body than a group of people who had common interests and tried at all costs to avoid the institutional stereotype: minutes, membership, publication. As I recall, we used to pride ourselves on its informal structure."

That looseness of structure does not help the historian to reconstruct the story with great detail! However, the things done and the associations made during the 1950s in that group were highly significant for the shape which the new Society would take, and it is important to review as much as can be reconstructed about what took place in those years.

The Forerunner of the Society

In the early 1950s, and perhaps even before that, seminary teachers of social ethics met as part of a group called Seminary Professors in the Practical Fields. The social ethicists tended to get swallowed up in that group and they soon sensed a strong desire to form an association of their own. Among those who were instrumental in the discussions leading to a separation from the larger group of teachers in the practical field were James Luther Adams, Das Kelley Barnett, John C. Bennett, E. Clinton Gardner, Karl Hertz, Henry E. Kolbe, Murray L. Leiffer, William H. Lazareth, Victor Obenhaus, Prentiss Pemberton, Liston Pope, John Satterwhite, Kenneth L. Smith, and Kenneth Underwood. Undoubtedly there were others who were active, but their names do not show up in the few documents that remain from the very early years. Most of the participants in that group felt a kinship of some kind with Walter Rauschenbusch and others of an earlier period who stressed the necessity for a social emphasis in Christian thought. Some felt that the use of the adjective "social" to modify the term "Christian ethics" involved a redundancy, but after heated discussion about the organizational name the advocates of including the term "social" won this round. Within a few years, however, the term "social" would be dropped from the title of the new Society.

The Edward W. Hazen Foundation of New Haven assisted the group with grants to support the travel costs of those attending its meetings. These grants were modest, but very helpful in the economy of that period. The first grant for $350.65 was made in 1950 and approximately that same amount was given to the old association almost every year through the decade of the 1950s. In fact, the Hazen Foundation continued to give travel money on into the 1960s to support the more formally organized Society.

The records of the meetings for this period are few and far between. There is a letter from Kenneth Underwood of the Yale Divinity School, dated March, 1953, that reports he was elected "president" (the more common phrase used of early leaders was "chairman") at a meeting held early in that year at Yale and indicating that the conference in 1954 would be held at Union Theological Seminary. Underwood's letter indicates that twenty-six persons were present at the Yale meeting, which decided, among other things, to initiate a critical and constructive study of the National Council of Churches' report on Christian ethics and economics which was to be published soon. There are no records of other aspects of the 1953 program.

The 1954 meeting at Union Seminary heard papers by both Reinhold Niebuhr and Liston Pope. A number of people remember this meeting because it was one of the earliest public appearances made by Reinhold Niebuhr after his stroke. Since copies of the program have not been discovered, little else can be reported. Oscar J. F. Seitz of Bexley Hall was elected chairman and Harold W. Fildey, vice-chairman and secretary of the Association.

The Association held its 1955 meeting January 21-22, 1955 at the College of Preachers of the Washington Cathedral. The theme for that meeting was "Preparing the Minister to Work Toward an Unprejudiced Society." Friday afternoon Frank D. Dorey of Howard University School of Religion gave an opening presentation on "The Dynamics of Prejudice." Harold W. Fildey of Oberlin and Murray D. Leiffer of Garrett responded. Friday evening, Samuel C. Kincheloe, of Chicago Theological Seminary, presented a paper on "The Local Church and Race Prejudice--Sociological Aspects" and Joseph F. Fletcher of Episcopal Theological Seminary and Karl H. Hertz of Hamma Divinity School responded. On Saturday morning the subject of the paper was "The Minister's Task--Pastoral Community Counseling" presented by Frank S. Loescher of Temple University. The discussion panel consisted of Albert T. Mollegan of the Protestant Episcopal Theological Seminary in Virginia and John H. Satterwhite of Hood Theological Seminary. The registration list shows that twenty-two persons were present at this meeting. A list to be used to make contacts with persons teaching in the field was drawn up. It consisted entirely of persons related to member schools of the American Association of Theological Seminaries.

The 1956 meeting was held at the Graduate School of Theology at Oberlin. The dates were April 27 and 28, the only time in the life of either the early Association or the subsequent Society which broke with the January pattern. Harold W. Fildey planned the program and hosted the meeting. The agenda of Friday afternoon and evening consisted of six presentations on the impact of various factors on Christian social ethics. Walter Marshall Horton of Oberlin spoke twice, once in the afternoon on the impact of theology, and the other time in the evening on the impact of historical studies. Walter W. Sikes of Butler University considered the impact of economics, and Karl D. Hertz of Hamma Divinity School, the impact of sociology. Edward L. Long, Jr. of Virginia Polytechnic Institute turned attention to the impact of current world trends, and Harold W. Fildey of Oberlin, to the impact of Group Dynamics Research on the discipline.

Saturday there were three papers and a panel. Lewis Smythe of the College of the Bible discussed "The Communication of Ethical Insight to the Laity"; Frank B. Lewis of the Union Theological Seminary in Virginia, "The Task of the Christian Social Ethics Professor with the Present Seminary Student Generation"; and E. Clinton Gardner of the Candler School of Theology, "Helping Seminary Students to Present the Idea of Christian Vocation." The panel, which was chaired by Victor Obenhaus of Chicago Theological Seminary, considered "The Present Status of Christian Social Ethics Departments in our Schools, and Ways to Improve the Understanding of our Students in this Field." Karl Hertz was elected chairman of the Association and assumed the main role in planning for the 1957 meeting that was held at the Western Theological Seminary in Pittsburgh, January 25 and 26.

At Pittsburgh, provision was made for early arrivals to have an informal "gossip session" (to quote the program) on professional problems. On Friday afternoon the main part of the program began with an analysis of the ways in which the organized church brings about change. The speaker was Harold C. Letts, Secretary of Social Action for the National Council of Churches. "The Local Community as a Scene of Social Change" was considered by a guest speaker, Elmer J. Thompson, Executive Secretary of the Health and Welfare Federation of Allegheny County. On Friday evening, John Bruere, minister of Calvary Presbyterian Church in Cleveland, spoke of "The Role of the Minister in Social Change," and Eleanor Rider, of the Commission of Human Relations of Pittsburgh, on "The Role of the Layman and Citizen." The use of guests, not members of the teaching profession as such, which appears for the first time in this 1957 meeting, was to become an important feature of many future programs.

Saturday morning Das Kelley Barnett of the Episcopal Seminary of the Southwest led the group on the subject "Theology and Ethics as Ways of Understanding the World and Communicating our Understanding"; and Albert T. Rasmussen, of Colgate-Rochester Divinity School, was scheduled to speak on "Theology and Ethics as Instruments for Motivating Social Action," but he had to cancel the engagement because of illness. The weekend was concluded with an informal roundtable on "The Educational Task Re-evaluated." John Satterwhite of Hood Theological Seminary was elected chairman and Culbert G. Rutenber of Eastern Baptist Theological Seminary, vice-chairman. Expected attendance at the Pittsburgh meeting was diminished because of bad weather.

In September of 1957 Culbert Rutenber wrote to John Satterwhite to say that everything seemed in order for the 1958 meeting at Eastern Baptist Seminary near Philadelphia, January 31 and February 1. (He also indicated that the room charge would be $1.50 and that the three meals would cost a total of $3.00!) The program as planned, however, suffered several last minute alterations. Edward Heimann of the New School for Social Research spoke to the first session on Friday afternoon on the subject "Christian Foundations for the Social Sciences." Heimann was substituting for Paul Lehmann, who could not attend. H. Richard Niebuhr of Yale gave the second address of Friday afternoon, dealing with the "Theological Basis of Christian Ethics." Kenneth Thompson addressed the group Friday evening. There is no topic indicated for Thompson's presentation, possibly because he was a last minute addition to the program. Kenneth Underwood of Wesleyan University closed the Friday evening period with a paper on "Protestantism, Politics, and Economic Policy."

On Saturday morning William Muehl of Yale spoke on "The Christian Citizen and Practical Politics." Kenneth Smith of Crozer, who had become involved in Pennsylvania politics, had tentatively secured Senator Joseph Clark, a three-term U.S. Senator from Pennsylvania, to speak to the group on Saturday morning. When Senator Clark was unable to keep the engagement, Kenneth Smith spoke in his stead on "The Theology of Politics."

Twenty names show up on the memo of registrations, though at least one of these had to cancel. The gatherings of the Association of Seminary Professors of Christian Social Ethics attracted about this number of people each year. This was not, however, a good representation of those teaching in the field at the time. Harold Fildey had made a list in 1954 of those teaching ethics either full or part-time in the seminaries of the United States and Canada and found a total of 127 names. Clearly, while the Association of Seminary Professors of Christian Social Ethics was having valuable programs and providing benefits to those coming, it was far from reaching the potential it ought to have had as a professional association. One of the people to see this most clearly was Das Kelley Barnett, who was elected at the 1957 meeting to chair the Association. The decision was made to hold the next meeting at Wesley Theological Seminary in Washington, D.C. in January of 1959, and Chairman Barnett spent many hours working toward making the 1959 meeting the founding session of the American Society of Christian Social Ethics in the United States and Canada.

The Founding Meeting

Considerable effort went into the preparation for the meeting that officially organized the American Society of Christian Ethics. Most of this effort was expended by Professor Barnett, who wrote to a list of over a hundred seminary teachers of Christian ethics and Christian social ethics to solicit interest in the founding of a new society and to encourage attendance. The response was quick and impressive, and more than fifty professors (all men and all teaching in seminaries) indicated they would plan to attend. Some names, such as that of Paul Ramsey who was already active in the group, are not found on the list used. While a general observation was made that teachers of Christian ethics in colleges were a source of potential membership for the new Society, there is no evidence they were systematically contacted and only those who happened to have other contacts knew about the effort to found the new society. Some forty other persons expressed regrets that they could not attend because of other engagements, but indicated a strong interest in forming such a society.

Nor was Chairman Barnett slack on other fronts. In addition to securing the renewal of the grant of $350 that the Hazen Foundation had regularly offered the Association to support the travel costs of its members attending the meeting, Barnett obtained a grant of $3000 from the American Association of Theological Schools to defray in part the cost of planning and holding regional meetings of the new Society during 1959 and 1960. Barnett also secured money from other sources--gossip had it that he knew wealthy oil tycoons in Texas--and the statement of expenses for the founding meeting in Washington lists a total of $586.35 from anonymous donors given for honoraria and the travel expenses of guest speakers at the meeting.

A printed program, quite similar to the one that has been used at most subsequent annual meetings of the Society, was prepared, though it bore the heading "The Annual Meeting of the Association of the Seminary Professors of Christian Social Ethics." Das Kelley Barnett gave what became, both in substance and in title, the first presidential address. It was devoted to the history of the life of the old Association and to the prospects for the envisioned society. Barnett stressed the need to make a more formal organization than had existed in the past. At the business meeting that followed, a consensus in favor of forming the new group was reached and the following decisions were made concerning its character: First, it was decided that the Society would be strictly professional; second, it was decided that the purpose of the Society would be to further the study and teaching of Christian social ethics; third, its aims would include promoting research in the history of Christian ethics, in theological and social ethics, in sociology and ethics, in comparative religious ethics, and also to promote the discovery of more effective pedagogical and research methods; fourth, membership would be open to men [sic] actively engaged in teaching social ethics and having professional training as well as to those now engaged in affiliated professions such as the departments of Christian social relations in various denominational and ecumenical organizations; fifth, the name of the group would be the American Society of Christian Social Ethics in the United States and Canada; and sixth, the annual dues would be five dollars.

Henry E. Kolbe of Garrett Biblical Institute was elected president of the Society and Frank B. Lewis of Union Theological Seminary in Virginia was elected vice-president. William H. Lazareth of Philadelphia Lutheran Seminary was elected secretary and treasurer. Das Kelley Barnett was designated executive secretary. The earliest governance arrangement consisted of regional directors, and those elected to these positions included Douglas E. Jackson of Perkins School of Theology, Albert T. Rasmussen of the Pacific School of Religion, Walter W. Sikes of Butler University School of Religion, Kenneth L. Smith of Crozer Theological Seminary, and E. Clinton Gardner of Emory University. The regional structure for governance was to be important for a brief time, but was later modified.

The program of the 1959 meeting consisted of two panels, and (as was to be the case for several years thereafter) arranged entirely in plenary sessions. This meeting pattern made it possible for everyone who attended to remain in one group and to think about the issues together. The first panel addressed the topic "A Christian Ethic for an Affluent Society." It was chaired by Douglas Jackson and consisted of John C. Bennett of Union Theological Seminary and two guests: Leon Keyserling, formerly chairperson of the President's Council of Economic Advisors, and Robert B. Wright, Chief, Economic Defense Division, Office of International Resources, Bureau of Economic Affairs, United States Department of State. The point of departure for the discussion was the book by John Kenneth Galbraith, *The Affluent Society* (Houghton Mifflin, 1958). The other panel was entitled "The Moderate's Strategy in Race Relations," and was chaired by John H. Satterwhite of Wesley Theological Seminary. E. Clinton Gardner of Emory University and Guy H. Ranson, formerly of the Southern Baptist Theological Seminary and at that time visiting professor-elect at Duke Divinity School, were participants in this panel from the Society's membership. They were joined by four guests: Robert R. Brown, Protestant Episcopal Bishop of the Diocese of Arkansas, Will D. Campbell of the Department of Racial and Cultural Relations of the Division of Christian Life and Work of the National Council of Churches, Brooks Hays, a member of Congress for a number of years and more recently a delegate to the Tenth General Assembly of the United Nations (1955), and W. Astor Kirk, former Legislative Assistant to Senator Earl Douglas and Professor of Government in the

Huston-Tillotson College in Austin, Texas. Each member of the panel presented some particular facet of the problem of segregation and how it could be ameliorated. The remarks of Guy Ranson were published in revised form in *The Kentucky Western Recorder* for July 16, 1959.

The First Annual Meeting

The numbering of the annual meetings of the Society designates each meeting by the anniversary of the founding. Hence, while the founding occurred in 1959, the first annual meeting was held January 29-30, 1960 at Union Theological Seminary in New York. Forty-two men attended from all regions of the United States and Canada, slept three to a room for $3.50 each at the Paris Hotel, and ate meals at the seminary "at prevailing prices."

John C. Bennett of Union Theological Seminary in New York was elected the new president of the Society and Frank B. Lewis of the Union Theological Seminary in Virginia was re-elected vice-president. Lewis Smythe of the College of the Bible was elected recording secretary. The work of the executive secretary was expanded to include the handling of funds, and Das Kelley Barnett of the Episcopal Theological Seminary of the Southwest was re-elected to the enlarged office of executive secretary. The policy of having regional directors was continued, and to the list that was elected in 1959, the names of C. Douglas Jay, Emmanuel College, Toronto, and Frank H. Gardner, Drake Divinity School in Iowa, were added. It was also decided to elect directors-at-large. James Luther Adams of Harvard, Joseph Fletcher of the Protestant Episcopal Seminary in Virginia, T. B. Maston of the Southwestern Baptist Theological Seminary, Paul Ramsey of the Department of Religion of Princeton University, and John H. Satterwhite of Wesley Theological Seminary were elected to these positions.

The program for the 1960 meeting centered largely on the teaching of ethics and did not include any guests from outside the discipline. A panel on Friday afternoon discussed the teaching of Christian ethics. Waldo Beach, of Duke Divinity School, Edmund Smith of Northwest Lutheran Theological Seminary, and Henry Stob of Calvin Theological Seminary were the participants. The most remembered part of the program was the address at the dinner meeting on Friday by Reinhold Niebuhr. One of those who was there writes, "He was not the old Niebuhr that I had heard many times when he visited Yale, but he went over his familiar themes and kindled the flames for social justice in us. I think this was his last time to address the Society, and it was a touching time for those who had known him and learned from him and his books and lectures." The Saturday morning session was devoted to a review of community projects organized by teachers of Christian social ethics and was led by Charles G. Chakerian of McCormick Theological Seminary and Lewis Smythe of the College of the Bible.

The annual meeting of 1960 did some preliminary planning for the regional meetings to be held within the ensuing year, using the grant of $3,000 secured for this purpose from the American Association of Theological Schools. The Board of Directors recommended that five such regional meetings be held. These regional conferences were to follow a format of three sessions. In one, the discussion was to center on the relationship of Theology and Christian social ethics, with a paper from either a member of the Society from the region or a visiting lecturer; in a second session, there was to be a discussion of various theological and practical problems in the field; in a third, attention would be directed to the methodology of teaching Christian social ethics, and materials such as course syllabi and bibliographies were to be exchanged.

The Regional Meetings

A Report on the regional meetings is included in a 1960-61 *Yearbook* prepared by the executive secretary. This mimeographed, spiral-bound document was some sixty pages in length and included a report on each of the regional meetings, a report of the second annual meeting, and a report on the growth of the Society. The year 1960 was one of the busiest in the Society's history and also one of the best documented.

The projected five regional conferences were reduced to four in number, each concerned with the broad rubric "Problems and Trends in the Teaching of Christian Social Ethics." Each of these regional meetings was planned by a regional director and hosted by a theological school. On March 11 and 12, 1960, the Perkins School of Theology was host to the Southwest region of the Society. Douglas Jackson made the arrangements. T. B. Maston of Southwestern Baptist Theological Seminary presented a paper "Teaching Social Ethics," the full text of which was printed in the *1960-1961 Yearbook*. Albert C. Outler of Perkins gave a paper on "Words from Theology to Teachers of Christian Social Ethics." Considerable discussion followed these papers concerning the place of social ethics in the seminary curriculum, the nature of Christian social ethics as a discipline, the responsibility of the teacher toward the church, the denomination, and the secular political order. The problem of dealing with students who strongly accept the status quo and look for pat answers from the church was also discussed.

Three other regional conferences were held in April of 1960. The first of these convened at Vanderbilt University, April 1 and 2. E. Clinton Gardner arranged this meeting and gave a paper on "Problems in Christian Ethics," which was concerned with the relationships between theology and ethics, with the difference between indicative and imperative modes for doing ethics, and with the contrast between the Christian and the secular orders. Gardner chided the church for its failure to deal effectively with economic, political, racial, and educational problems of the time. In reporting on the Nashville meeting, Theodore Weber, also of Candler, indicated that several considerations dominated the proceedings. A great deal of attention was devoted to defining the nature and scope of the discipline, particularly on how to obtain precision and clarity with terminology and how to relate the sociology of religion to the theological disciplines. The proper role of the Christian social ethicist was discussed, particularly the relative importance of being an academician and being a social activist. The problem of communicating with those who do not hold to the Christian faith was raised, as were issues of curriculum design. There had even been a long discussion of the most appropriate format for such meetings themselves. Weber concluded his report by indicating there had been a widespread feeling at the Nashville gathering that the regional gatherings were more productive than the annual meeting because they were smaller in size and hence facilitated better discussions. They were also more unified and less disjunctive than the sessions of the national group.

Another regional gathering was held April 22 and 23 at Emmanuel College in Toronto, and professors from Anglican, Baptist, Presbyterian and United Church theological colleges in Canada participated. C. Douglas Jay was the planner and convener. Two papers were presented at the Toronto meeting. The first, by William Morris of Huron College, evaluated four theological positions foundational to Christian social ethics. These four positions included biblical theology (Barth, Brunner), liberalism (Rauschenbusch), neo-orthodoxy (Reinhold Niebuhr), and paleo-orthodoxy symbolized by the Incarnation rather than by the Cross. Morris himself defended the fourth position. The second paper, by Prentiss Pemberton of Colgate Rochester Divinity School, was entitled "The Importance of the Behavioral Sciences in the Development of a Social Ethic." Pemberton suggested that the Church's resources of worship, doctrine, and responsive love must be related to, and supplement, the reasoned insights of the behavorial sciences. Two discussions, one led by Donald Wade of Knox College and the other by Arthur Boorman of United College in Montreal, dealt with specific problems of course design, syllabi construction, bibliographical matters, and involvement in community activities. Like the Nashville meeting, this meeting made known its strong preference for the regional gathering.

The fourth of the regional meetings was held at the Garrett Biblical Institute, Evanston, the last weekend in April. Thirteen professors from the Middle West attended. This meeting was chaired by Henry E. Kolbe. Paul Elman, of Seabury-Western Theological Seminary, gave a paper dealing with the contrast between an ethic of principle and contextual ethics. While the paper made no effort to resolve the thorny issues between these two approaches, the minutes indicate it "elicited considerable discussion." Walter W. Sikes, of Butler School of Religion, gave a paper using the population issue as a case study of a social problem. He based the paper on the book by Richard Fagley, *The Population Explosion and Christian Responsibility* (Oxford University Press, 1960). This meeting, as all of the others, engaged in "shop talk" and in discussion of the field. Syllabi were exchanged between members, and problems of defining the field of Christian social ethics were canvassed.

Both the Nashville meeting and the Toronto meeting took great pains to note the attractiveness and usefulness of the regional meeting idea. But it seems that even as their accolades were made, the obituary was all but written. The practice of having regional meetings was soon abandoned, undoubtedly with the exhaustion of the grant funds from the American Association of Theological Schools. Only a Pacific Coast section would, some years later, meet regionally--and that largely because the difficulty and cost of travel precluded many members teaching on the West Coast from getting to the annual meetings that were generally held east of the Mississippi. Like shrubs that grow rapidly and blossom profusely, these regional meetings undoubtedly raised hopes but did not prove to be enduring. They may well, however, have given the fledgling national society a needed boost at a critical period in its life.

The Second Annual Meeting

The program of the second annual meeting of the Society, which was held at Garrett Biblical Institute on January 27 and 28, 1961, was practically identical in format to the meetings of the Association of Seminary Professors as well as to the 1960 meeting of the Society. Friday afternoon President John Bennett presided over a symposium on "Religion and the Political Order, 1960." E. Clinton Gardner of Emory University, T. B. Maston of Southwestern Baptist Seminary, and George W. Forell of Chicago Lutheran Theological Seminary were present and presented papers.

G. McLeod Bryan of Wake Forest College and John W. Turnbull of the Episcopal Theological Seminary of the Southwest could not attend but submitted papers that were included in *The Yearbook*, along with the papers by Gardner, Maston, and Forell.

The presidential address by John C. Bennett was entitled "Ethical Principles and the Context." Bennett's address was later published, slightly revised, as a chapter in the book *Storm Over Ethics* (United Church Press, and Bethany Press, 1967:1-25). The book was a response to the publication of Joseph Fletcher's *Situation Ethics* (Westminster Press, 1966). It is interesting to see that a presidential address given to the Society in 1961 was pertinent to a controversy that reached its zenith five years later.

Saturday morning Joseph Fletcher was scheduled to give a presentation on "The Use of the Case Method in Teaching Christian Social Ethics," but he was unable to attend. The time was given to Paul Ramsey's presentation of "The Just War and the Nuclear Dilemma." Professor Ramsey has indicated that his presentation was work in progress for a chapter in the book edited by John Bennett, *Nuclear Weapons and the Conflict of Conscience* (Charles Scribner's Sons, 1962), and was some version of his "Hatfield and McCoys" parable.

In the business meeting on Friday evening, E. Clinton Gardner of the Candler School of Theology was elected president, Kenneth L. Smith of Crozer Seminary was elected vice-president, and Das Kelley Barnett was re-elected to the post of executive secretary (and treasurer). The office of recording secretary dropped out of the listing. It was relatively easy in those days to juggle such matters since there was as yet no constitution for the Society. Not content to let contextualism win over institutionalism on such a matter, the Society made efforts following the 1961 meeting to produce a constitution embodying its statement of purpose and by-laws. The "regional directors," as they continued to be called, for 1961-62 were John C. Bennett, Robert E. Fitch, Douglas E. Jackson, Henry E. Kolbe, T. B. Maston, Victor Obenhaus, Paul Ramsey, John H. Satterwhite, Walter W. Sikes, and Donald V. Wade. Without the strictures of a constitution it was also comparatively easy to blur the distinction between regional directors and directors-at-large, so a differentiation considered very important the previous year was casually laid aside.

There was no doubt that at the end of two years of existence the Society was alive and well, giving promise for the future. The membership by this time numbered 117. Ninety-six of these were teachers in theological schools or on faculties of divinity. The remaining twenty-one were either teachers in college or university departments of religion, executives in denominational agencies or social action groups, or undesignated. The exclusive grip of theological education on the identity of the Society had been broken.

The story of the life and work of the Society that followed the events reported in this chapter is told in the next two parts of the book. The three chapters which constitute Part Two deal with the growth of the Society and treat among other things: the demographic, religious, and sexual characteristics of its membership; its leadership; its financing; the dates, places, and formats of its annual meetings; the work of its special interest groups and task forces; and actions which the Society has taken on matters affecting its own life or the larger world of scholarship. These details help us to understand who composed the Society, how it has managed its affairs, and the impact it has had on American scholarship, on the wider public life, and on the religious situation in America.

Part Three, consisting of six chapters, gives a detailed report on the substantive content of the programs of the annual meetings. The primary arrangement within this part is by topics. Both the theoretical (or foundational) issues that have been discussed in papers given before the Society and specific social problems that have been addressed on the programs are reported. The chapters, each of which contains one or more topics, are ordered according to the frequency with which the papers dealing with the subjects they discuss appeared on the programs. For instance, the largest number of papers dealt with various foundational issues--hence those issues are discussed first. Within each of the topics the arrangement is basically chronological, so that changes in the approach to various subjects across the years can be appreciated.

The account of the programs is fairly complete, though clearly it has not been possible to report on all of the papers and panels in the same detail. Papers that have not been located by the search for materials are mentioned by author and title in the appropriate place. In the case of papers that have been printed for general distribution, either in the Society's own publications or elsewhere, usually only the gist of the paper is given, since those wishing to have a fuller grasp of the content of such papers can follow the bibliographical documentation to the printed version. Presidential addresses, even though most of them are available either in the archives or in a printed form, are discussed a bit more fully since the Society has always granted them a special visibility. In the case of papers that are available only in the archives, a somewhat fuller synopsis of the paper is usually given because it is not possible for the average reader easily to secure the original. Interestingly enough, there are no papers available from the 1959 and 1960 meetings and only one from the year 1962. In contrast, the archives are complete for the years 1961, 1967, 1968, and 1969. A good proportion of the papers given in each of the other years is available, considering the difficulty of collecting materials so long after they were presented. Even though it has been impossible to gather a total record, it has been possible to construct a reliable and informative account of the issues to which the Society has paid attention.

Part Four of this book consists of an interpretive analysis of the Society's achievements and the role it has played in relation to Christian ethics and Christian social ethics in America. It briefly considers the directions in which the life of the Society may move in the next period of its activity.

Part Two
Morphology

2

The Society's Growth: A Statistical and Logistical Overview

Many members of the Society--they might even constitute a majority--would probably hold that "small is beautiful" and that a state of "no growth" is something to be strongly advocated. But no such frame of mind operated in planning for the third annual meeting. In the spring of 1961 Paul Ramsey sent a memo to the members of the Society reporting on the second annual meeting and urging members to propose papers as well as to suggest names of persons to be solicited as possible new members. In those days the problem in devising the program was not, as it has been in more recent years, to winnow down a plethora of proposals, but to solicit sufficient interest. Ramsey found it necessary to solicit the membership a second time for response to this request. In the second memo he penned this memorable admonition: "In order for the program to be arranged and for authors to be able to include the summer months in their time for preparation, please review whether you have made the response you should make to this request or the one permitted by 'your stations and its duties.'" Ramsey's diligence apparently bore fruit, for a rather full program emerged and the growth of the Society was launched.

Once the growth of the Society began it became a significant and steady process. The growth of the Society has been modest in comparison with the growth of groups like the American Academy of Religion (formerly the National Association of Biblical Instructors) over the same period. But it has been sizable in comparison with that of invitational discussion groups, like the American Theological Society, which deliberately limit their size in order to insure that meetings can be held in plenary session. While the growth of the Society has resulted in some loss of the small group intimacy which was felt in the very early years, it has not caused the Society to become too large for true collegiality to be experienced at its meetings. Indeed, many members of the Society find its meetings a welcome contrast to the whirl of larger gatherings of professional associations with which many of them are also related.

There has been a bit of talk over the years about forming a second group--one more selective in its requirements and more directed in its agenda. Such a group might recapture some of the intimacy that once characterized the meetings of the Society itself. However, nothing has come of this, a fact that in itself witnesses to the extent to which the growth of the Society has not seriously destroyed its collegial quality.

Another fact that indicates how much the collegial quality of the Society has stayed intact despite the growth has been the degree of interest which its members have shown in its governance. Attendance at the annual business meeting is generally as high as that at any of the plenary program sessions. While the final arranging of the program has been done by an executive group, most other decisions about the Society's life have been made or fully reported in open deliberations to all those coming to the annual business meeting. The Society is not a perfect democracy, but it is a far cry from a highly centralized bureaucracy.

Membership Statistics and Characteristics

In 1960-61, Das Kelley Barnett, the executive secretary, prepared what seems to be the first membership roster. This provides the best available source of the demographic characteristics of the Society in its early years. In most subsequent years, members were given a mimeographed list of names and addresses of all members. More recently, it has been the customary practice to provide each member with a moderately readable machine copy of a computer printout of the same data. (There has never been a directory that contains biographical or occupational information.) Much can be ferreted out from these materials concerning the growth and membership demographics of the Society. The 1960-61 roster lists 117 members. From similar lists done in succeeding years, we learn that in the next five years the membership increased to 140; in the next five years to 319; in the next five years to 491; in the penultimate five years to 603; and in the final four years to the 664 for 1983. The smallest percentage growths have been in the first five and in the last four years. Each year some members have dropped out and a relatively few have died, but the new additions have been more than sufficient to sustain an increase. With an increasing number of members reaching the golden years there will probably be more losses in the next twenty-five years than there have been in the past, and with the shrinking of educational enrollments and programs it may be harder to find a cadre of replacements in the future. The devotees of "no growth" may yet be satisfied.

The most incontrovertible thing that can be learned from the membership lists is the geographical distribution of the membership. A comparison of the geographical distribution of the 1960-61 list with the 1983 printout is given in Table One. (p. 20) This table reveals some very interesting facts about the Society and presumably also about the profession it brings together. The percentage of the membership located in New England, in the Middle and South Atlantic states, in the Northern Midwest and in the Western plains and mountains has not changed more than three or four percentage points either way during the first twenty-five years of the Society's existence. The biggest shrinkage in the percentage distribution of members has been in the Southern Midwest, where the proportion of members has decreased in percentage by more than half.

There is nothing in these statistics that suggest Christian ethicists--or at least those attracted to join the Society--have the Sunbelt urge, or that (like textile factories) they are forsaking the Northeastern regions of the country for places where the prerequisites of productivity can be obtained more cheaply. Perhaps the tendency of the Society to hold its meetings more often in the Middle Atlantic States has made it more appealing to those living in this area than to those elsewhere--but that would be difficult to prove. The biggest comparative gain in membership has been in the Pacific Coast group, which has grown nearly threefold. Still, this area now accounts for only about ten percent of the Society's total membership. There are only nine states that are missing from both lists. These are: Alaska, Arizona, Hawaii, Idaho, Montana, New Mexico, North Dakota, Utah, and Wyoming. The Canadian membership has stayed almost constant at just over four percent. A very small group located overseas maintains membership in the Society.

It is more difficult to be precise about some other factors that characterize the membership of the Society. But highly informed estimates are possible. As we have noted, the Society was an outgrowth of a group located almost entirely in theological seminaries or on faculties of divinity. In 1960-61 ninety-one of the 117 members were still so located, thirteen were teachers in colleges or university departments of religion, eight held executive positions in denominational or other kinds of social agencies, and the occupational identities of five cannot be placed. By the end of the fifth year of the Society's existence, the dominance of teachers in theological schools had clearly begun to erode. Of the 170 members in 1965, the number

TABLE ONE
GEOGRAPHICAL DISTRIBUTION OF MEMBERSHIP

	1960-61		1983	
	N	%	N	%
New England				
Connecticut	4	3.42	13	1.96
Maine	1	.85	4	.60
Massachusetts	7	5.98	35	5.27
New Hampshire	-	.00	2	.30
Rhode Island	-	.00	4	.60
Vermont	-	.00	1	.15
Subtotal	12	10.25	59	8.88
Middle Atlantic				
Delaware	-	.00	1	.15
Dist. of Columbia	2	1.71	37	5.57
Maryland	1	.85	10	1.50
New Jersey	5	4.27	25	3.76
New York	8	6.84	51	7.68
Pennsylvania	9	7.69	44	6.63
Subtotal	25	21.36	168	25.29
South Atlantic				
Florida	1	.85	13	1.96
Georgia	8	6.84	12	1.80
North Carolina	6	5.13	19	2.86
South Carolina	-	.00	2	.30
Virginia	1	.85	23	3.46
Subtotal	16	13.67	69	10.38
Northern Midwest				
Illinois	14	11.97	43	6.47
Indiana	1	.85	32	4.82
Iowa	3	2.56	9	1.36
Kansas	-	.00	3	.45
Michigan	3	2.56	18	2.71
Minnesota	1	.85	27	4.07
Ohio	3	2.56	26	3.92
West Virginia	-	.00	6	.90
Wisconsin	-	.00	12	1.80
Subtotal	25	21.35	176	26.50
Southern Midwest				
Alabama	-	.00	3	.45
Arkansas	-	.00	1	.15
Kentucky	6	5.13	13	1.96
Louisiana	2	1.71	2	.30
Mississippi	1	.85	-	.00
Missouri	4	3.41	17	2.56
Oklahoma	2	1.71	3	.45
Tennessee	3	2.56	11	1.66
Texas	11	9.40	24	3.61
Subtotal	29	24.78	74	11.14
Western Plains and Mountain States				
Colorado	-	.00	5	.75
Nebraska	-	.00	2	.30
South Dakota	1	.85	4	.60
Subtotal	1	.85	11	1.65
Pacific Coast				
California	4	3.42	61	9.19
Oregon	-	.00	2	.30
Washington	-	.00	7	1.06
Subtotal	4	3.42	70	10.55
Canada	5	4.27	28	4.22
Overseas	-	.00	9	1.36

teaching in seminaries or on faculties devoted to training clergy had dropped to about ninety. In contrast, by the same year nearly forty members taught in colleges or university departments of religion. By the year 1983 more members of the society were teaching in university or college settings than in theological schools. This constitutes a major shift in the professional orientation of many of these teaching in the field, and clearly suggests that the field of Christian ethics is no longer the sole province of theological education.

There is no such clear-cut change in the number of members giving specialized leadership on church boards, in other social action agencies, or in "think tank" type situations. Whereas in the early years there were less than ten, there are now somewhere around seventy. This increase is roughly proportional to the growth of the Society as a whole.

In its earliest years the Society was predominately male, white, and Protestant. The 1960-61 list contains the name of only one woman. There were two women by 1964-65; twenty by 1976; and by 1983 there were over fifty women in the Society. While this does not remotely approach equality between the sexes, it does represent tangible progress toward opening the field to women. In contrast, there were six Blacks in the 1960-61 group, but there are only about fifteen in the 1983 group. This means that, proportionately, the Blacks have suffered a decrease in representation.

One of the exciting things in the life of the Society, which began roughly at the time of Vatican II, was the coming into its midst of Roman Catholic moral theologians. A handful first attended the meetings of the Society in 1963, during which year six of them became members. The presence of Roman Catholic clerics during the middle sixties was obvious, since they were still wearing distinctive garb, but this practice has waned considerably in the seventies, not infrequently because individuals have been laicized. Beginning with the year 1965, Roman Catholics joined the Society at the rate of five or six per year through the sixties. By 1970 over thirty had joined, including one woman. Many of the Roman Catholics who joined the Society in the sixties have subsequently served as officers. In the seventies the size of the group joining each year became larger, so that by 1975 there were 83 or more members of the Society with Roman Catholic identities, including five women. About 145 can be found on the 1983 roster. The growth of Roman Catholic membership, once it began, has been roughly proportional to the growth of the Society as-a-whole.

The Society has welcomed into its membership an occasional Jewish scholar who has worked in Christian ethics, but the number of such cases has been less than half a dozen.

During its history the Society has made a number of modifications in how the conditions of membership first proposed at its founding are to be stated. The conditions of membership require high professional competence in the field, as shown in an earned doctorate or some equivalent evidence of intellectual attainment in the subject. The first debates concerning the appropriate way to phrase the requirement occurred in 1968. The section of the bylaws which had read "A prerequisite for membership is evidence (such as an earned doctor's degree, experience, position of responsibility, or writing), which indicates competence in the critical analysis of Christian ethics and social problems" was changed to read "A prerequisite for membership is either an earned doctorate or scholarly publications in the above named fields [i.e., in Christian ethics or social ethics]". In 1974 the question of eligibility requirements was again vigorously debated, particularly to insure that no arbitrary exclusions were being unwittingly made. This time the applicable bylaw was rephrased to read "A prerequisite for membership is at least one of the following: A Ph.D. or equivalent degree, scholarly publications, or a full-time teaching position in ethics and/or related fields in an accredited institution."

In the view of those defending the change, who carried the vote, this provision maintained the spirit of the tradition that membership in the Society should be open only to those actively and competently working in the field in a scholarly way, yet allows appropriate flexibility to the Board in electing members with special or with unusual backgrounds. The 1974 change has not radically altered the nature of the membership. However, when passed it did enable thirty-eight applicants who would have been barred from membership by a strict application of the old wording, to be voted in immediately after it was passed, and others in subsequent years.

Clearly the sentiment of the Society has always been to stress intellectual and academic competency as the major qualification for membership. This has kept a certain tone to the Society. Indeed, going to one of its meetings means rubbing shoulders with a very large portion of the most active and productive scholars and figures in the discipline. One observer has noted astutely: "Whereas in some professional settings you talk about those who are writing in the field, at the Society of Christian Ethics you talk with them."

In 1964 the question of admitting graduate students was raised and the next year the board recommended a bylaw change to provide for such a class of members. In 1968 the bylaw condition for student memberships was reconsidered and a time limit added. The resulting provision was made to read: "Doctoral students in ethics who have passed their general (comprehensive) examinations may be members of the Society for not more than three years." In 1978 this provision was changed to make five years the limit. The distinction between regular and student members has never been sharply drawn, and affects bookkeeping and dues setting rather than the privileges accorded members at meetings. Indeed, the category of any particular individual does not even appear on the address list distributed to members annually, nor is there any differentiation in the activities possible in the life or deliberations of the Society.

The bylaws also provide that "life membership may be granted without payment of dues, upon their retirement from full-time employment, to those who have been members of the Society for at least ten years."

Governance and Officers

While the Society was founded in 1959, it was not until two years later that efforts were initiated to draw up a documentary phrasing of its purpose and specific guidelines for its operation. The first set of bylaws was adopted in 1964, at which time the American Society of Christian Social Ethics in the United States and Canada became simply the American Society of Christian Ethics--its name until 1979.

One of the consequences that resulted from organizing the Society more officially in 1964 was to lose the annual grant of $350 that for a number of years had been provided by the Hazen Foundation to encourage individuals to attend the annual meeting by subsidizing their travel expenses. Otherwise, things continued to be done much as they had been. The bylaws as written describe the operations of the Society quite accurately. They are consulted from time to time--mostly when the outcome of some deliberation might be affected by the manner in which a decision is reached. These bylaws act like a constitution but can be changed somewhat easily in response to circumstances or to perceived inadequacies in the existing rules. There is seldom resistance to such changes; there are few strict constructionalists among the membership. The bylaws can be amended by a majority vote of the annual meeting providing the proposed amendment has been "included in the call for the meeting, or was submitted at the previous annual meeting, or is recommended by a two-thirds vote of the Board of Directors." It is not difficult to get one or more of these conditions met.

The Society has never been legally incorporated, though

it rather early took the necessary steps to be designated by the Internal Revenue Service as a group to which contributions are tax deductible.

The bylaws provide for the following elected officers: A president, whose duties include presiding over meetings and customarily delivering an address to the membership at the annual meeting; a vice-president, who since 1963 has been the president-designate and who functions in case the president is unable to do so; twelve directors, each elected for a term of four years (two of which are chosen to serve on the executive committee that plans the annual meeting); and an executive secretary, who normally serves four years, acts as treasurer, collects dues, sends out notices of meetings, and does most everything else routinely or unexpectedly required to keep the Society functioning smoothly.

The process for electing these officers involves a nominations committee which brings a slate to the floor. The chairperson of the committee is a member of the Board of Directors and four other members of the Society who are not members of the Board, serve with the chairperson. For many years the nominating committee was constituted only as the annual meeting began and did its work in cloakrooms, at meal times, and (late at night) in someone's hotel room. In recent years the process has become far more deliberate. The membership of the committee has been designated in advance of the meeting, has looked carefully at possibilities, and has come to the meeting with a number of ideas already canvassed. This helps to insure that persons who are not able to attend the meeting for some legitimate reason are not excluded from consideration. In the earlier years the nominations committee presented a slate of nominees only sufficiently large to fill the vacancies, and nomination was tantamount to election--even though the theoretical possibility of nomination from the floor always existed. At the 1975 meeting there were two nominations from the floor for positions on the Board of Directors and a real contest ensued. It was directed by a motion made at that meeting that in the future twice as many nominations would be presented for membership on the Board as there were vacancies to be filled--a practice that has been followed since 1976. Beginning with the 1977 meeting, two candidates have been named for the position of vice-president (president-designate) and each year since some eminently qualified person has tasted the bitterness of seeing another member of the Society get the greater number of ballots. This deference to the principle of democratic choice has been accompanied by efforts to provide those voting with better biographical information, but seldom have any policy issues--which give election choices their greatest significance--been at stake.

Table Two chronologically lists the presidents, vice-presidents, and executive secretaries who have held office since the founding of the Society. The presidents have included two Blacks, one woman, twenty teachers in seminary, five teachers in college/university departments of religion, and one person working in a center for policy studies.

TABLE TWO
CHRONOLOGICAL LISTING OF OFFICERS

Year Elected	Presidents	Vice Presidents	Executive Secretaries
1959	Henry E. Kolbe	Frank B. Lewis	Das Kelley Barnett*
1960	John C. Bennett	Frank B. Lewis	Das Kelley Barnett
1961	E. Clinton Gardner	Kenneth L. Smith	Das Kelley Barnett
1962	Paul Ramsey	Kenneth L. Smith	Das Kelley Barnett
1963	Walter W. Sikes	Prentiss L. Pemberton	Das Kelley Barnett
1964	Prentiss L. Pemberton	Paul Elmen	E. Clinton Gardner
1965	Paul Elmen	Victor Obenhaus	E. Clinton Gardner
1966	Victor Obenhaus	Murray Leiffer	E. Clinton Gardner
1967	Murray Leiffer	James Luther Adams	E. Clinton Gardner
1968	James Luther Adams	James Gustafson	Douglas Sturm**
1969	James Gustafson	John H. Satterwhite	Douglas Sturm
1970	John H. Satterwhite	Charles Curren	Douglas Sturm
1971	Charles Curren	Edward L. Long, Jr.	Douglas Sturm
1972	Edward L. Long, Jr.	Charles C. West	Franklin Sherman
1973	Charles C. West	Roger L. Shinn	Franklin Sherman
1974	Roger L. Shinn	Preston N. Williams	Franklin Sherman
1975	Preston N. Williams	J. Philip Wogaman	Franklin Sherman
1976	J. Philip Wogaman	Waldo Beach	Max L. Stackhouse
1977	Waldo Beach	Walter G. Muelder	Max L. Stackhouse
1978	Walter G. Muelder	Donald W. Shriver, Jr.	Max L. Stackhouse
1979	Donald W. Shriver, Jr.	Douglas Sturm	Max L. Stackhouse
1980	Douglas Sturm	Daniel C. Maguire	Joseph L. Allen
1981	Daniel C. Maguire	Beverly W. Harrison	Joseph L. Allen
1982	Beverly W. Harrison	Thomas W. Ogletree	Joseph L. Allen
1983	Thomas W. Ogletree	Alan Geyer	Joseph L. Allen
1984	Alan Geyer		

*In the first year the positions of executive secretary and secretary-treasurer were separate. William H. Lazareth was elected secretary-treasurer in 1959.
**Douglas Sturm assumed office August 1968.

The Board of Directors includes all elected officers and the elected directors plus (since 1972) the chairperson of the Pacific Coast section, and (since 1981) the editor of the *Annual* who attends without vote. The incoming board assembles near the conclusion of each annual meeting (usually at a ghastly early hour on Sunday morning) and plans for the conduct of affairs during the forthcoming year. The main meeting of each board immediately precedes the annual meeting, at which time it makes those decisions it is empowered to make under the bylaws and goes over the items that will be on the agenda of the annual business meeting, frequently making recommendations for consideration by the whole membership.

Table Three alphabetically lists those who have been directors of the Society and the years of their service. Of the 85 persons who have been directors, serving a total of 257 years, ten have been Black, serving a total of 41 years, and eight have been women serving a total of 32 years. (These figures presume the completion of the designated term of each incumbent.) Almost three times as many directors have been associated with seminaries as with colleges or university departments of religion and less than half a dozen have served in social agencies or on denominational boards of social concern.

The Board enjoys certain designated powers, which include the right to vote qualifying applicants into membership, the right to set minimum dues, the power to authorize expenditures, and the power to act on all matters of policy and program between the yearly business meetings. Over the years the Board has been very careful to inform the membership of actions it has taken and has listened with great care to the desires of the membership about matters of program and policy. It is also the duty of the Board to have accounts regularly audited and to provide a report on the audit to those attending the annual business meeting. The fees related to the annual meeting (registration, housing, meals, etc.) are decided by the executive secretary in consultation with the chairperson of the committee of local arrangements.

All other powers reside in the membership attending and voting at the annual meeting. A quorum for the annual business meeting long stood at twenty-five but in 1978 was raised to fifty in light of the increased size of the Society. There has never been any difficulty raising the required quorum to do business--even at the rare occasional Sunday morning adjourned sessions needed to handle a special matter.

The Pacific Coast Section

A good example of the manner in which bylaw changes have been made in response to developments in the life of the Society is found in the story of the Pacific Coast section which was organized in the early 1970s. A group of sixteen members of the Society, all but two of them living in Southern California, met together at La Casa de Maria near Santa Barbara on December 7, 1971 for the exchange of professional reflections and the discussion of means to facilitate more regular professional interaction among themselves. Unsure of the ASCE's attitude toward having a regional section, they also considered associating with the Western section of the American Academy of Religion. David Wills was appointed chairman of the group and John Orr vice-chairman. Edward Long, Jr. then vice-president of the Society, was present at this gathering.

TABLE THREE
SERVICE RECORD OF DIRECTORS

A single date indicates election to a one year term as regional director or director-at-large (designations used until 1962); a hyphenated date indicates election to a specific term, usually four years; an asterisk means the individual resigned while a director to accept another office in the Society.

James Luther Adams	1960
Joseph L. Allen	1962-64
Terence R. Anderson	1974-78
Henlee Barnett	1962-66
Robert C. Batchelder	1963-67
Waldo Beach	1962-63
John C. Bennett	1961,1962-66
James Bresnahan	1981-85
Elizabeth Bettenhausen	1980-84
J. Arthur Boorman	1970-74
John Boyle	1980-84
Charles Brown	1979-83
Lisa Cahill	1983-87
Frederick Carney	1968-72
James Childress	1972-76
George H. Crowell	1977-81
Charles Curran	1966-70
Paul K. Deats	1973-77
Roland Delattre	1975-79
Riggins Earl, Jr.	1981-85
Paul Elman	1963-64*
Margaret Farley	1974-78
Robert E. Fitch	1961
Joseph Fletcher	1960,1967-71
E. Clinton Gardner	1959,1960 & 1962-66
Frank E. Gardner	1960
Alan Geyer	1967-71
Paul Geren	1962-64
Robert Gessert	1969-73
James Gustafson	1964-68
Marlene Halpin	1971-75
Stanley Harakas	1983-87
Stanley Hauerwas	1982-84
Beverly Harrison	1976-80
Paul Harrison	1964-68
Dieter Hessel	1976-80
Douglas Jackson	1959,1960,1961
C. Douglas Jay	1960,1965-69
Major J. Jones	1976-80
Henry E. Kolbe	1961
Karen Lebacqz	1982-86
Robert Lee	1964-68
Murray Leiffer	1962-63
Edward Long, Jr.	1964-65,1965-69
Harold Lunger	1963-64
T. B. Matson	1960,1961
Richard McCormick	1972-73
Daniel Maguire	1969-73,1975-79
James Nelson	1982-86
Kieran Nolan	1970-74
Victor Obenhaus	1961
June O'Conner	1979-83
Enoch Oglesby	1980-84
Thomas Ogletree	1978-82
Peter Paris	1977-81
Allan M. Parrent	1973-76
Prentiss Pemberton	1962-64
Ralph Potter	1978-82
John Raines	1981-85
Paul Ramsey	1960,1961
Larry Rasmussen	1983-87
Warren Reich	1965-69
Charles H. Reynolds	1973-77
Daniel Rhoades	1967-71
Isabel Rogers	1978-82
John Satterwhite	1960,1961 & 1962-65
Harvey Seifert	1962-63
Franklin Sherman	1979-83
Roger Shinn	1972-75*
Donald W. Shriver	1973-77
Walter W. Sikes	1959,1960,1961 & 1962-63*
Kenneth L. Smith	1959,1960
Andrew N. Spaulding	1971-75
Max Stackhouse	1968-72
Glen Stassen	1974-78
Douglas Sturm	1963-67
John Swomley	1966-70
Donald V. Wade	1961,1962-65
Joseph Washington	1969-73
Theodore Weber	1968-72
Charles C. West	1966-70
Preston N. Williams	1970-74
Gayraud Wilmore	1975-79
J. Philip Wogaman	1971-75
John Howard Yoder	1977-81

It was the thinking of the West Coast group that at least one item emerging from their deliberations might well be included in papers distributed annually by the Society, that a line be put in the Society's budget on a regular basis for the partial support of a section, and that the chairperson or other designated representative of the section should become a member of the Society's Board of Directors. David Wills attended the 1972 annual meeting of the Society and presented this case to the board and to the members. The bylaws were changed to accomplish most of these objectives.

The second annual meeting of the West Coast section was held in December of 1972. Vice-president Charles West attended. To cover his expenses, the small amount designated for the section in the general budget was supplemented by honoraria associated with speaking engagements arranged to coincide with his visit. The program for this meeting consisted of one panel and four papers.

By 1974, the Pacific Coast section, now chaired by William W. May, had a membership of approximately seventy-five people. In that year it scheduled its gathering in May to coincide with a visit from President Roger Shinn. In 1975 Stuart McLean became the representative of the Pacific Coast section and served in that capacity three years. Other representatives have been: Donald E. Miller, 1978; Clark Kucheman, 1979-1980; Robert Blaney, 1981, and Anthony Battaglia, 1982 and 1983.

It has not always been possible to arrange a visit by one of the national officers, particularly when air fares were proportional to mileage. The 1981 meeting of the Board of Directors discussed the matter and concluded that the West Coast section should arrange lectures or find other means of financing the trip if it expected a visit from the president of the Society as a regular part of its activities. The presence of the West Coast group was, of course, exceedingly important to the Society in 1979, when it held the regular annual meeting in Los Angeles.

The case of the Pacific Coast is unique. No other section of the country has proposed to arrange sectional gatherings.

Meeting Places, Size, and Format

Table Four indicates the locations and January dates of each of the annual meetings of the Society. The most popular location has been Washington, D.C. For many years the halls of Wesley Theological Seminary seemed almost like a "home away from home" to the Society's members. More

TABLE FOUR
MEETING LOCATIONS

Founding	Wesley Theological Seminary	Washington, D. C.	Jan. 30-31, 1959
1st	Union Theological Seminary	New York, New York	29-30, 1960
2nd	Garrett Biblical Institute	Evanston, Illinois	27-28, 1961
3rd	Southern Baptist TS	Louisville, Kentucky	26-27, 1962
4th	Southern Baptist TS	Louisville, Kentucky	25-26, 1963
5th	Wesley Theological Seminary	Washington, D. C.	24-25, 1964
6th	Wesley Theological Seminary	Washington, D. C.	22-23, 1965
7th	Garrett/Seabury Western	Evanston, Illinois	21-22, 1966
8th	Wesley Theological Seminary	Washington, D. C.	20-21, 1967
9th	St. Paul School of Theology	Kansas City, Missouri	19-21, 1968
10th	Wesley Theological Seminary	Washington, D. C.	24-26, 1969
11th	ITC and Gammon TS	Atlanta, Georgia	23-25, 1970
12th	Wesley Theological Seminary	Washington, D. C.	22-24, 1971
13th	Bergamo Center	Dayton, Ohio	21-23, 1972
14th	Richmond Theological Center	Richmond, Virginia	19-21, 1973
15th	Windemere Hotel	Chicago, Illinois	18-20, 1974
16th	University of Tennessee	Knoxville, Tennessee	17-19, 1975
17th	National 4-H Center	Washington, D. C.	16-18, 1976
18th	Toronto School of Theology	Toronto, Ontario	14-16, 1977
19th	National 4-H Center	Washington, D. C.	20-22, 1978
20th	Davidson Center, USC	Los Angeles, California	19-21, 1979
21st	Union Theological Seminary	New York, New York	18-20, 1980
22nd	Iowa Memorial Union	Iowa City, Iowa	16-18, 1981
23rd	National 4-H Center	Washington D. C.	15-17, 1982
24th	Essex Hotel	Indianapolis, Indiana	14-16, 1983
25th	Philadelphia Centre Hotel	Philadelphia, Pennsylvania	20-22, 1984

recently, when the size of the Society and the other commitments of Wesley made it impossible to continue meeting there, the National 4-H Center became almost as familiar a territory. Other East Coast meetings include two held at Union Theological Seminary in New York and one scheduled for Philadelphia in 1984. In contrast to the twelve meetings held on the East Coast, the Society has met ten times in the Midwest, three times south of the Mason-Dixon line, once in Canada and once on the West Coast. In the early years, on-campus accomodations were usually provided by host academic institutions, but at recent meetings hotels and/or conference centers have been used instead. More seminaries than colleges or universities have acted as host institutions. For about six years the last weekend in January was the customary date for the meeting, but it has since been moved forward to the third weekend of the month. For eight years the meeting was only two days (one intervening night) long, but then it was made three days in length. The coldest receptions from the weather standpoint occurred in Toronto and in Iowa; the warmest, in Atlanta and Los Angeles. One of the unexplained mysteries is how Wesley Seminary was so often able to turn on a warm winter sun just for the meeting.

Table Five indicates structural features of the meetings and points to the changes in format that have occurred over the years. While the actual duration of the meetings has about doubled (not including the pre-meeting sessions of the board), the number of participants on the programs has increased approximately fourfold between the first ten year and the last ten-year average. There are many reasons for this increase in the number of program participants. More members have joined the Society; over the twenty-five-year period, educational institutions have become more and more gratified to have members of their faculties visibly involved in the program; finally, more and more subject interest areas have opened up for exploration. When the Society went to the West Coast, it had an all time high of one hundred eleven members formally involved in the meeting--not least, one suspects, to help as many as possible to qualify for travel grants from their institutions.

Clearly the meetings of the Society have changed from the gathering of a reasonably intimate group consisting of three or four plenary sessions in which everyone was involved, to the meeting of a larger and more diverse professional guild gathering for both plenary and concurrent sessions. The introduction of the concurrent seminar idea in 1965 and its significant expansion in the 1970s was the device by which the participation in the meetings of the Society was opened to a much larger number of participants without a major lengthening of the meeting time. Another device used to increase significantly the number of persons on the program was to appoint designated moderators in advance of the meeting and list their names on the program.

The expansion of the meeting occurred in a series of small steps. It never seemed like a momentous matter to add a session to the meeting schedule in any particular year. But most of the additions became permanent features of the program and were seldom offset by cutbacks. The addition, in 1972, of the book discussion sessions has proven to be one of the most popular parts of the program. Through 1983 the Society has taken note in this fashion of the appearance of 141 books in the field, not infrequently with the author of the book being discussed present at the session. The program has often, but not always, made use of panels to address particular issues. As more panels have come to be used in the concurrent sessions somewhat fewer have been evident in the plenary groups. Although the various interest groups held meetings informally for a number of years during the annual meeting it was not until 1977 that their gatherings were listed on program.

TABLE FIVE
FORMAT OF ANNUAL MEETINGS

	Plenary Portions of Meeting				Concurrent Sessions								
Year	Number of Plenaries *	Papers Given *	Respondents	Panels	Format +	Papers	Panels	Book Dis-cussions	Scheduled Interest Groups	Guests on Program	Conveners or Moderators	Worship Services	Total Participants On Program
1959	3	1	–	2	–	–	–	–	–	8	5	–	16
1960	3	1	–	2	–	–	–	–	–	1	–	–	7
1961	4	3	–	1	–	–	–	–	–	1	–	–	7
1962	8	7	2	–	–	–	–	–	–	1	5	–	17
1963	10	10	–	–	–	–	–	–	–	–	2	–	13
1964	10	10	2	–	–	–	–	–	–	–	2	–	13
1955	6	5	3	1	1 with 3	4	–	–	–	5	2	–	16
1956	6	5	–	2	2 with 2	–	2	–	–	3	3	–	20
1967	6	4	2	2	1 with 5	**	1	–	–	2	3	–	33
1968	6	7	8	2	–	–	–	–	–	3	7	1	24
1969	6	4	6	2	1 with 4	3	1	–	–	3	11	1	35
1970	3	4	2	1	3 with 3	7***	4	–	–	11	13	–	37
1971	5	8	4	–	1 with 4	7	2	–	–	6	9	1	38
1972	5	4	2	1	1 with 5	9	2	10	–	4	9	–	50
1973	3	4	3	–	2 with 2 2 with 2 1 with 3	8	1	9	–	7	10	–	36
1974	4	3	4	1	4 with 3	11	2	14	–	2	13	–	65
1975	4	4	2	1	4 with 3	15	–	16	–	6	15	–	66
1976	3	3	2	–	2 with 4 2 with 5	17	1	16	–	3	20	–	62
1977	3	2	1	1	4 with 5	19	1	15	5	3	24	1	76
1978	3	1	–	2	4 with 5	19	1	10	7	3	22	1	62
1979	3****	2	1	1	4 with 6	24	1	10	5	1	31	1	111
1980	3	2	2	1	4 with 6	24	1	11	7	3	24	1	79
1981	3	2	2	1	4 with 5	20	–	9	6	7	32	–	67
1982	3	3	4	–	4 with 6	25	–	10	9	4	39	–	81
1983	3	3	4	–	4 with 6	24	1	11	10	2	38	–	84

NOTES: *These figures include the annual banquet and the Presidential Address
**At this meeting the concurrent sessions were based upon discussions of eleven previously distributed papers.
***More than one paper was read at a single concurrent session.
****A fourth plenary session, immediately following the Annual Business Meeting, was devoted to a twenty-year history of the Society.
+The first figure represents the number of times concurrent sessions were scheduled and the second figure the number of sessions that met each of the times.

When a plenary Sunday morning session was first included in the program, care was taken to arrange an ecumenical worship service. This often came early on Sunday and was not always well attended. With the enthusiasm in the late sixties for "religionless Christianity" and with the pressure to use the full Sunday morning hour for an outstanding plenary, the worship was dropped after a few years. It was resumed again between 1977 and 1980, but has again disappeared. This is the one feature of the program which, although once started, has not had a subsequent steady place on the agenda.

One of the unusual features of the programs over the years has been a steady flow of guests invited to address or to take part in the deliberations of the Society. There have been about ninety such guests in the twenty-five years. They have been invited to come for many different reasons. One group has been asked to come because its philosophical or theological accomplishments have attracted much attention and the membership has welcomed the opportunity to meet them in person. Among others, this group has included (in chronological order) Will D. Campbell, Reinhold Niebuhr, Robert O. Johann, John L. McKenzie, Bernard Hàring, Jùrgen Moltmann, Jon M. Lochman, C. Eric Lincoln, Rubem Alvez, J. Deotis Roberts, John Mbiti, Max Wartosky, Denis Goulet, Gregory Baum, Herbert Richardson, and Elisabeth Schussler Fiorenza. Another group might be described as persons of affairs, people whose accomplishments in political, ecclesiastical, or economic life have attracted the attention of members of the Society. At the founding meeting in 1959 Leon Keyserling, former chairman of the President's Council of Economic Advisors; Robert B. Wright, Chief of the Economic Defense Division, Office of International Resources, Bureau of Economic Affairs, U.S. Department of State; Brooks Hays, former representative for the Fifth District of Arkansas; and W. Astor Kirk, legislative assistant to Senator Paul Douglas, were present. In the 1960s the guests included Benjamin Payton, director of the Community Service Project in Washington; Hyman H. Bookbinder of the Office of Economic Opportunity; Louis Joughlin, associate secretary of the American Association of University Professors; Nathan Wright of the Department of Urban Work, the Episcopal Diocese of Newark; and Marshall W. Nirenberg, chief, Laboratory of Bio-chemical Genetics, National Heart Institute. In the 1970s the group included Vincent Harding of the Martin Luther King Center in Atlanta; Charles E. Spivey, Jr., executive director of the Department of Social Justice, National Council of Churches; a reappearance of Benjamin Payton; James Lawson of Memphis, Tennessee (of civil rights fame); Geno Baroni, Center for Urban Ethnic Affairs, Washington, D.C.; Joseph M. Davis, Executive Director, National Office for Black Catholics; Ronald Goldfarb, a Washington lawyer who was previously with the U.S. Department of Justice; Justice Patrick Hart of the Supreme Court of Ontario; Congressman Robert Drinan; and the Stated Clerk of the United Presbyterian Church, William P. Thompson.

A fourth group of guests has consisted of academicians from other fields whose work bears in some way on ethics and whose insights are considered useful to the work of the members of the Society. Included in this group have been biblical scholars Paul W. Meyer and John L. McKenzie; William V. O'Brien of the Institute of World Polity, Georgetown University; John E. Lynch of the School of Canon Law, Catholic University of America; Jφrgen Randers, associated with the Club of Rome Report; Edward Pellegrino, Yale University, speaking about biomedical ethics; Ronald Mueller, the American University in Washington, dealing with problems of world development; Donald Saliers of Emory University, speaking about liturgy; and Sister Isabel Letelier, of the Institute for Policy Studies in Washington, dealing with liberation thought in the Third World. Among the economists we have heard in the 1980s, are Robert Leckachman of Lehman College, Harvey H. Segal of Citibank, Jerome Kurtz and William Tabb of Queens College.

On two occasions the Society has devoted a special session to the thinking of a well-known figure and asked that figure to be present and to respond to the presentations made by members of the Society. Hannah Arendt was present for this purpose at the Sunday morning plenary session of the 1973 meeting; William Frankana, in 1975.

Finances

Table Six (p. 34) gives a composite picture of the financial expenditures of the Society over its history. Every year a financial report has been distributed to the membership at the annual meeting. The categories under which expenditures have been listed have shifted a bit from time to time, and the table has tried to take this fact into account for purposes of comparison. The financial picture has been a healthy one, thanks both to skillful work on the part of executive secretaries and to a steady step-by-step increase in the dues. From the time of founding through the first decade, the membership dues remained at a steady $5.00 per year. They were then raised to $10.00, at which level they remained until they were raised to $15.00 in 1976. A sliding scale of dues, setting amounts according to salary

TABLE SIX
COMPARATIVE EXPENDITURES

Year	Total Spent	Cost of Annual Mtg. Program	Paper Dist.	Ex Sec'y Salary	Office Costs	Program Planning	Membership Fees	CSR Delegates	Task Forces	History	Section Support	Misc.	Balance
1961f	1,161.35	593.86	-	-	567.49	-	-	-	-	-	-	-	329.28
1962	no record												
1963f	703.06	302.05	-	-	243.26	157.75	-	-	-	-	-	-	360.33
1964p	381.75	44.29	-	-	161.60	175.86	-	-	-	-	-	-	unclear
1965f													
940.49	399.46	152.72	100.00	160.06	128.25	-	-	-	-	-	-	(16.99)	
1966f	1,357.06	713.35	215.71	200.00	188.00	40.00	-	-	-	-	-	-	372.44
1967f	1,113.41	267.20	191.40	250.00	216.02	173.64	-	-	15.15	-	-	-	225.23
1968f	1,074.50	428.21	unclear	250.00	471.29	50.00	-	-	-	-	-	-	(30.50)
1969c	1,336.33	296.11	132.36	250.00	172.90	33.45	-	-	326.51	-	-	-	(70.33)
1970c	1,679.55	780.61	unclear	250.00	319.96	128.00	86.98	-	114.00	-	-	-	2,045.75
1971c	3,349.48	997.65	185.02	500.00	208.67	243.08	640.63	353.57	220.86	-	-	-	(490.50)
1972c	3,846.52	614.31	392.02	500.00	701.37	290.91	650.00	565.64	133.27	-	-	-	1,454.17
1973c	5,538.61	1,300.74	246.12	500.00	1,288.38	303.47	1,092.50	499.82	102.58	-	-	25.00	708.76
1974c	5,261.22	1,847.06	unclear	1,000.00	1,401.43	485.80	122.13	177.20	-	-	-	227.50	(1,985.87)
1975c	7,304.44	2,016.77		1,000.00	1,506,98	584.15	1,280.25	221.02	300.00	-	-	123.00	(1,819.23)
1976c	5,381.96	1,126.35		1,000.00	1,195.40	422.51	1,400.00	133.45	-	-	100.00	4.25	3,309.01
1977c	7,758.37	2,069.75		1,200.00	1,473.62	738.72	1,465.63	550.65	200.00	-	50.00	10.00	86.77
1978c	6,387.59	1,921.52		1,200.00	890.15	202.05	1,628.25	435.14	-	100.38	-	-	1,854.73
1979c	9,494.34	3,476.74		1,200.00	1,217.37	567.41	2,080.77	452.66	356.24	118.15	-	25.00	(450.52)
1980c	10,163.34	695.14	2,292.48	1,200.00	1,849.78	1,026.72	2,143.76	648.68	291.78	-	-	15.00	1,494.91
1981c	10,995.10	65.00	3,449.18	1,500.00	1,328.09	1,258.02	2,208.27	701.79	157.50	-	269.25	18.00	(74.41)
1982c	10,305.24	368.20	3,090.28	1,500.00	1,280.46	1,262.34	2,316.64	380.69	50.50	56.03	-	-	1,532.91

EXPLANATIONS: The letter "f" after the year indicates fiscal year--meeting date to meeting date; the letter "p" indicates a partial year; and the letter "c" indicates calendar year.

In 1974 and 1975 the expense for lodging and meals of the annual meeting were included in the financial report distributed to the membership. These are excluded here for comparison purposes.

This table corrects an error of $3.00 in the financial report distributed in 1974.

The amount indicated for the annual meeting in 1961 includes $443.86 distributed to members as travel subsidies.

The amount shown under Task Forces for 1975 was a grant to The Religious Studies Review.

levels, was instituted in 1981. In 1983 it was decided, effective with the billing for 1984, to add another step at the top of the sliding scale, making the present dues structure as follows:

Students and others without salary	$ 6.00
Salaries up to $19,999	18.00
Salaries $20,000 to $29,999	21.50
Salaries $30,000 to $39,999	25.00
Above $40,000	30.00
Retired members (dues paid at least ten years)	no fee

When it was proposed to add the additional step at the top, the executive secretary estimated that there would be very few members affected by the highest bracket.

The Society has also increased its income over the years by charging a registration fee for the annual meeting. When first instituted in 1966 this fee was only $2.00. It has increased over the years and in recent years has been $15.00 for members, $18.00 for non-members. The only other substantial income of the Society has been from the sale of its publications and from interest on the balances in its savings accounts.

By far the greatest proportion of its expenditures has been for the logistical support of the Society's own operations, though when the Society joined the Council on the Study of Religion at the beginning of the seventies it took on a considerable additional financial responsibility. That responsibility may also be characterized as logistical support for the ongoing operations of a professional group.

The Society has not provided any large amount of financial support to ethical inquiry or the productive work of individual scholars. It did make a grant of $300 in 1975 to help launch *The Religious Studies Review* and in 1983 a grant of $500 to the new *Journal of Law and Religion*, but these were extraordinary gestures. It has given modest support to task forces committed to the examination of some problem or issue. Unless it seeks and obtains funds for the purpose, the Society is not likely to be significantly involved in the direct financial support of productive scholarship by individuals or small groups. But over the years it has found several other ways of providing encouragement and support to ethical reflection and to cooperate with other professional societies or public interest groups in action and reflection. In the next two chapters we will look at those achievements.

3

The Internal Productivity of the Society: Publications, Task Forces, and Interest Groups

This chapter examines several ways in which the Society has fostered scholarship and inquiry among its members and found ways to disseminate the results of that work to a wider scholarly community. It tells two stories: the first, about the extensive efforts across the years to launch some sort of publication, either under the auspices of the Society or as a direct consequence of its efforts; the second, about the creation from time-to-time in the life of the Society of special interest groups or task forces to probe an issue, to pursue some particular concern, or to concentrate the Society's attention on some particular responsibility.

Efforts to Undertake Publications

A ditto sheet in the files indicates that at the business session of the Society on January 27, 1961 (for which there are no minutes) a motion was introduced as follows; "The American Society of Christian Social Ethics shall undertake the publication of a journal of Christian ethics exhibiting a quality and depth comparable to that of *Zeitschrift für Evangelische Ethik,* to be issued quarterly, and supervised by an editorial board selected both from members of the ASCSE and from leading figures in the field of Christian ethics in this country and abroad." To initiate this project it was further moved that funds (not less than $15,000 to start) be solicited and that a journal committee be appointed to organize an editorial board.

The idealistic hopes embodied in that motion have been something of a visionary goal throughout the entire history of the Society, and a great deal of dedicated service has gone into efforts to bring about some form of regular publication under the Society's sponsorship. None of these efforts, however, has brought forth quite the kind of journal envisioned by the resolution quoted in the previous paragraph. Throughout the years the discussion of publications has been a perennial feature of the meetings of both the Board of Directors and the membership as a whole. Perhaps no other single category of business, unless it be bylaw changes dealing with the Society's name or conditions for membership, has received as much attention.

In 1964 the Board of Directors, less visionary in its hopes, talked about the possibility of establishing a *Newsletter* for the Society, to be published two or three times a year. While the annual business meeting, on the board's recommendation, passed a motion to implement such an activity, no such instrument was forthcoming on a regular basis in the subsequent months. In 1965 the discussion revolved around the possibility of publishing a yearbook, perhaps in cooperation with The Society for the Scientific Study of Religion, but no action on this idea was taken. Along the way a committee was appointed to consider again a possibility of publishing a journal in the field of ethics. This study group reported to the Board of Directors at the 1967 meeting. Its report called for the appointment of another committee (a) to prepare a specific plan for an annual volume, (b) to investigate the several publications that carry articles and monographs in social ethics, and (c) to report to the executive committee by April 1, 1967 with specific recommendations. This time the Board meant business! The executive committee of the Board was empowered to look at the report and then to canvass the membership as a whole for a decision regarding publication without waiting for the next annual meeting. The membership was to indicate by a mail ballot to be returned within twenty days whether to adopt the idea with a concurrent increase in dues, whether to disapprove, or whether to delay action until the 1968 Annual Meeting.

The committee appointed on the basis of this recommendation was chaired by Paul Deats, with James Gustafson, Gordon Kaufman, and Max Stackhouse as members. It did not exercise the option to begin publishing but reported first to the Board and then to the membership at the 1968 meetings. It recommended that a new committee be appointed to secure the funding for the kind of journal being envisioned and, if this funding effort was successful, that a new committee be formed to make a recommendation concerning editorial staffing. According to the minutes of the annual business meeting, the returning committee was "in essence recommending the publication of the annual proceedings of the Society."

The new committee called for by the old committee was chaired by Max Stackhouse, with Edward Duff, James Gustafson, and Prentiss Pemberton as members. It gave an intensive and carefully prepared report to the 1969 meeting of the Board. This report was more hesitant in tone and modest in its proposals, and spoke of the need for some sort of bibliographical publication. The minutes indicate "the committee was undecided exactly what procedure to follow to implement the idea." After protracted and inconclusive discussion by the board, including the idea that the publication efforts should be limited to the preparation of bibliographic studies, Max Stackhouse is reported as noting, "At least no one questioned the desirability of a bibliographic publication." Stackhouse is also recorded as having suggested that a committee might be appointed to pursue the matter further.

The 1969 board did not let the matter rest. It asked Warren Reich to invite a representative of *Corpus Instrumentorum* to attend an adjourned session of the Board, and by the very same evening Warren Reich obliged by introducing Harold C. Gardiner, editor of Corpus Books, with whom a friendly interchange followed. Afterwards, the Board acted on a motion calling for the incumbent and incoming presidents to appoint a publication committee having power to act (with the permission of the executive committee) to get some publication going "so long as such action entailed no substantial [financial] responsibility on the part of the Society." The new committee was also mandated to solicit the cooperation of foreign scholars and scholars not in the Society. When this action of the Board was reported to the whole membership at the annual business meeting, many suggestions came forth from the floor in the course of approving the action. None of these suggestions from the floor, however, shed much light on how a committee with the power to act could be expected to bring forth a significant achievement while deprived of the right to incur expenses.

The committee that was appointed in 1969 under the chairmanship of Warren Reich, demonstrated that a publications committee could do more than return with a recommendation that another committee be appointed. Reich, along with committee members Charles West and James Childress, worked hard on a number of fronts between the 1969 and 1970 meetings. The primary focus of its efforts was on cultivating bibliographic studies in various aspects of Christian ethics and finding a publication outlet for such studies. The committee proposed to the Board in 1970 that two editors, one from the Catholic and one from the Protestant tradition, be appointed, with modest honoraria, and it mentioned a number of possible avenues of publication, including a new journal that was being planned in the field. Edward L. Long, Jr. and Preston Williams were proposed for membership on the committee. Long accepted the assignment. A budget item of $400 was allocated for the use of the committee, which became officially the Editorial Board on Bibliographic Studies in Christian Ethics. The journal mentioned in the report was being planned at the University of Tennessee by a group headed by Charles Reynolds and it would be known as *The Journal of Religious Ethics*. It did not contemplate being directly sponsored or sustained by the Society, but it did ask for the Society's active encouragement and interested consultation.

Within a year the editorial board was able to report that a bibliographical essay on Black studies had been prepared by Shelby Rooks of Princeton and Henry Mitchell of Bexley Hall/Colgate Rochester Divinity School. A year later it could report the prospects of even more bibliographic essays. Its work received the gratitude of the Board of Directors and a mandate was given to continue another year.

A public announcement of the launching of *The Journal of Religious Ethics* was made at the 1973 meeting. Its editors were to be Charles Reynolds and Roland Delattre of the University of Tennessee, Arthur Dyck of Harvard, and Frederick Carney of The Southern Methodist University. All were members of the Society, as were ten of the fourteen members of a proposed advisory council. A motion to automatically include a subscription to this new publication in the dues structure of the ASCE was defeated and a substitute motion to applaud the establishment of *The Journal* and publicize it in mailings to members was passed with enthusiasm. While the new publication was not to be directly sponsored by the Society, its members were encouraged to subscribe and were offered a special introductory rate as an inducement for doing so promptly. *The Journal* was planned to have a selected theme for emphasis in each issue and to include, as available, bibliographical studies of interest to persons in the field of religious ethics. Moreover, it was a promising avenue for the publication of the bibliographical essays on which the editorial board of the Society was working.

Warren Reich presented a written report indicating progress with the development of bibliographical essays and noting the publication of one by James F. Childress on nonviolent resistance and direct action in *The Journal of Religion* for October 1972. The composition of the editorial board was changed. Warren Reich remained its chairman, with Frederick S. Carney, Robert M. Veatch, Stanley Hauerwas, and Alan Anderson named as the members.

The year 1974 saw the editorial board reporting on continued work on some thirty bibliographical essays and the publication of four. Warren Reich resigned as chairman and appreciation was expressed for his many years of service. Charles Reynolds became chairman and served for two years.

The concerns for publication covered not only materials generated by members of the Society but also ways to make papers from the meetings available to members. Prior to 1975 the papers selected from the annual meeting had been distributed in mimeographed form to members by mail after the meeting. Duplicating and mailing these papers had long been an onerous task for the executive secretary. Beginning in 1975 those papers from the annual meeting selected for distribution were printed in a neat paper bound volume called *The Selected Papers*, which was produced by the Scholars Press at the University of Montana. While this arrangement relieved the executive secretary of considerable work, the editorial preparation of the papers and putting them into camera ready form remained a large burden.

The year 1975 was also the year in which plans for the publication of *The Religious Studies Review* were announced, with James Gustafson as editor of the ethics section. The Board voted to support that new publication with a one-time grant of $300.

By 1976 the editorial board became known again as the publication committee. It reported that a bibliographical essay on Black theological ethics by J. Deotis Roberts had been published and that all the other essays either had not been finished or had been rejected. It was decided to cease encouraging the preparation of more bibliographical essays. Little of importance appears about publication in the minutes of the next three years except some talk about commissioning a history of the Society--first contemplated for the twentieth anniversary. The main thing to report is that beginning in 1977 *The Selected Papers* started to be printed on the equipment of the Council of the Study of Religion instead of by The Scholars Press.

At the 1980 meeting, Douglas Sturm submitted a written proposal to revise *The Selected Papers* to become *The Annual of the American Society of Christian Ethics*. According to Sturm's proposal, *The Annual* would be composed of at least four sections: selected papers from the annual meeting, bibliographies, course descriptions, and reports from task forces of the Society. Those attending the annual business meeting voted unanimously to establish this new procedure and to empower the Board to proceed towards publication, beginning with the appointment of a three-person publications committee. The first annual was published in 1981 and was edited by Thomas Ogletree, with assistance from Alan Anderson and Lisa Cahill. The 1981 Board received a report of the publication committee calling for certain changes in the bylaws to provide for the appointment of an editor for *The Annual* for a three-year term and to provide for an editorial board of four persons. With the new structure in effect Larry Rasmussen was appointed to a three-year term as editor of *The Annual* and Lisa Cahill to a one-year term on the editorial board, Alan Anderson to a two-year term, David Hollenback to a three year term, and Peter Paris to a four-year term. In 1982 Jane Cary Peck replaced Lisa Cahill and in 1983 Robin Lovins replaced Alan Anderson.

In 1981 it was pointed out to the Board that the cost of producing and mailing *The Annual* would go up considerably in 1982, and that the costs of travel for the editor to attend the annual meeting would also increase. The Board decided to keep the pattern and size of *The Annual* the same for 1982, but to have the executive secretary bring to its 1983 meeting a projection of expenses contemplated for the next two or three years. It may be quite difficult to continue the publication and distribution of this valuable aspect of the Society's work without significant readjustments of some sort.

The Society's encouragement of publication took on a new venture in 1983. A *Journal of Law and Religion* was being planned, bringing to fruition hopes of many members of the task force on Ethics and Law. The new venture asked for help from the Society towards founding costs. The Board agreed to provide a one-time grant of $500 and also to extend to the new journal the same courtesies which were extended to *The Journal of Religious Ethics* at the time of its founding.

No one could have foreseen, when the original idea of publishing a journal patterned after the *Zeitschrift für Evangelische Ethik* was conceived, the many different directions in which the publication efforts of the Society would move. Some may feel that the seeming inability of the Society to develop a highly visible, consistently formated, and traditionally conceived journal has been a major failure. Others will feel that the different patterns that have been devised have served the profession well. Whatever the fate of the Society's own offical publication plans, individual members have consistently taken their place in the ranks of those publishing materials useful for the advancement of the discipline.

Task Forces

One of the most productive instruments for doing the work of the Society has been the appointment of a group of members to inquire into some particular issue or to undertake some special inquiry. In some cases these have been called "interest groups" and in other cases "task forces," but it is not until the Board minutes of 1981 that the difference between them was explicitly articulated. According to those minutes: "interest groups are formed at the initiative of groups of members and are assigned a time slot at the annual meeting, usually Friday night after the presidential address. Task forces usually meet at the same time and in addition are budgeted funds by the Board, report to it, and ordinarily do not continue as task forces beyond three years." The constitutional warrant for having task forces and interest groups stems from the president's power to appoint "other committees."

The first task force to be formed was constituted by the tenth annual meeting, when Alan Geyer asked the Society to consider sponsoring a Consultation on Theological Education and International Affairs. The president was empowered to appoint the membership of a task force to pursue this matter, and the group was given expense money up to $50.00 and asked to report back in a year. In 1970 the group indicated that the matter of funding such a consultation was still being pursued. In yet another year it had given up trying to obtain funding for the special event but had arranged and produced a special issue of *The Christian Century* (April 23, 1969) on the subject. The task force was dissolved with thanks and Alan Geyer was commissioned to serve on a continuing basis as a liaison person with groups interested in the study of international affairs.

The second task force to be formed by the Society came about in response to a motion from the floor at the annual meeting in Atlanta in 1970. This motion called for the creation of a Task Force on White Racism. Its purposes were (1) to explore what it means to be a white Christian ethicist, (2) to share and develop strategies and tactics to combat white cultural and intellectual racism in educational institutions, and (3) to share and develop course designs to understand and combat white cultural and institutional racism. The discussion which preceded passage of this motion indicated that some members did not understand its import and that others had doubts about its advisability. Robert Terry was subsequently appointed chairman of this group and the members were Robert Batchelder, William Charland, Henry Clark, George Crowell, Donald Shriver, David Snider, and Glen Stassen. Preston Williams agreed to serve as a consultant.

This task force reported at the 1971 meeting and indicated plans to develop a more aggressive anti-racist attitude in the Society, "while acknowledging the basic scholarly function of the ASCE." These plans included five recommendations: (1) that the Society announce its intention to transcend a stance of "color blindness" and engage in a deliberate struggle to deal with the meaning of being Black or white humans; (2) that the Society call its members to attack racism within their respective spheres of influence and power; (3) that it encourage its members to develop the needed skills for doing these things; (4) that it include in its annual meeting an opportunity to report how some of its members have done so; and (5) that it encourage research and the writing of articles about this agenda. The task force was asked to compile and distribute at the next annual meeting course materials germane to this undertaking. It was commissioned to award up to four stipends of $50.00 each to members of the Society wishing to attend training conferences aimed at developing skills of the appropriate sort, and it was asked to plan a major session on these matters for the 1972 program.

The program planned for 1972 included a paper by Robert Terry and a panel led by Henry W. Clark. Both were placed under the rubric "Reflections on White Racism." Also during 1971 and 1972 some members of the task force attended a conference on white consciousnes, did research on White racism, prepared a bibliographic essay on the issue, and disseminated information to many persons seeking it. It considered sponsoring regional two-day conferences in teaching methods, but these did not materialize. As a result of its experiences, and prompted to do so by a paper prepared by Norman Faramelli, the group became interested in the broader issue of how action and reflection are related in social change. When a motion to create an interest group on action/reflection models was introduced, the Task Force on White Racism gave its support and ceased to exist. (The work of this committee or, as it became, interest group on action/reflection is discussed in the next section).

The third task force to be related to the Society came out of a motion presented by an *ad hoc* group of members at the 1971 annual meeting. The motion expressed concern over the implications of the Harrisburg conspiracy trial of Father Philip Berrigan and others--particularly over the possible effect of the trial on academic freedom and civil liberty. The motion put the Society on record, acknowledging those indicted to be persons of moral integrity and personal courage, but not as prejudging the legal issues. Instead, the motion asked that a way be found to "undertake, through the creation and funding of a special task force, to investigate this trial, to report to [the Society's] members the moral issues of this trial, and to prepare deliberations for the next Society meeting on the moral issues of civil disobedience and the use of the law to stifle political dissent in America."

Many members of the Society, including the spokesman who presented the motion on behalf of the *ad hoc* group (who here writes autobiographically), were concerned with how to balance concern about the issues with the scholarly stance of the Society. The minutes of the meeting show that this problem was resolved by interpreting the mandate of the task force to be one of advising the membership about the issues and what appropriate actions they might take as individuals rather than of taking public stances on the Society's behalf.

President Charles Curran appointed Edward L. Long, Jr., the vice president of the Society, to chair the task force and to appoint its membership. It was further stipulated by the Board of Directors that the expenses of the task force would be funded up to an amount of $200 and that the task force should not accept any money for its work from partisan or advocacy groups.

Almost immediately after the annual meeting, Long wrote to the entire membership of the Society, enclosing a copy of the resolution and asking those so inclined to suggest how the study should be conducted and what issues it should address. His letter also invited interested members to volunteer their services. Thirty persons responded, several of them indicating that they had no suggestions to make. Three members of the Society expressed doubts about the wording, intention, or legitimacy of the resolution. Sixteen made some general observations and eight of those sixteen offered some sort of help. Two other letters (each of which apologized for its brevity!) gave major substantive suggestions and a careful analysis of the issues. Eventually, about a dozen members of the Society worked on different aspects of the issues, with coordination by two sub-chairmen, James Childress and John Raines. Al Denman, James Johnson, and Larry Rasmussen produced written materials to be used. The three foci of the investigation were: the trial itself; the bearing of the trial on civil liberties; and the problems faced by individuals who come to feel protest beyond the normal limits of dissent is a burden of conscience.

Dieter Hessel, of the Department of Church and Society of the United Presbyterian Church in the U.S.A., brought some members of the task force together with interested persons from certain church and ecumenical agencies for a consultation that was held in June 1971 at the Krisheim Conference Center near Philadelphia. Extensive conversations were held and the materials generated from those conversations became the foundation for a paper prepared by Edward Long, Jr., that was published in pamphlet form as "Occasional Paper Number 7 of the Presbyterian Department of Church and Society" under the title *U. S. vs. the Harrisburg 8: Conspiracy Prosecution for Illegal Dissent*. Free copies of this pamphlet were made available by the Presbyterian Church to members of the Society.

The Society's task force also arranged for the Sunday morning program at the 1972 meeting, when the problems related to the trial were looked at by Professor Thomas Emerson of the Yale Law School, and Ronald Goldfarb, a Washington attorney who once had worked for the U. S. Department of Justice. This program concluded the work of this task force.

At the 1973 annual business meeting, Dieter Hessel introduced a proposal to establish a task force on the Ethical Dimensions of the Nation's Bicentennial Observance. Concerned that the bicentennial would be used to legitimize a self-congratulatory binge of civil religion, the movers of the motion asked that a task force be appointed by the president to (1) disseminate to members of the Society bibliographical and curricular information on the history of, and prospects for, the American Revolution: (2) explore the need for and author research papers dealing with critical ethical issues involved, and (3) recommend and help plan pertinent sessions for the 1974 and 1975 programs at the annual meetings. This task force began its work without budgetary support. (It was known that a number of denominational groups were interested and able to finance the process.) The task force that was appointed was chaired by Dieter Hessel, with the following members: Harry R. Davis, James Finn, Ronald Green, Allan Parrent, Donald Shriver, Ralph Smelzer, Preston Williams and David Wills. James Smylie of the faculty of the Union Theological Seminary in Virginia attended some of the sessions at which the idea of the task force was discussed and indicated that The American Society of Church History might possibly be interested in collaborating on this undertaking. John Howard Yoder also indicated that the Mennonites might possibly be interested.

Hessel reported to the 1974 board meeting that the task force was proposing that the ASCE join with the ASCH and an ecumenical task force coming from church groups to plan a three-day conference to be held at Princeton early in 1976 on the theme "Religion and Revolution Internationalized." To facilitate cooperation, a planning group of four (composed of Dieter Hessel, Allan Parrent, Gayraud Wilmore, and Charles West) was named and a budget of $200 provided from Society funds. At the business meeting, in response to questions from the floor, it was made clear that the Society's sponsorship of the Princeton meeting would not be allowed to interfere with the scheduling of the annual meeting of the Society for that year. There was also talk about having a special conference in Washington immediately prior to the annual meeting of the Society, but plans for that never materialized. There is no report in the Society's minutes of the subsequent work or disbanding of this task force.

The next task force to be established came into being at the 1976 meeting and was concerned with the relationships between law and ethics and law and theology. This task force has given a complete and careful account of its work over the years in the 1981 *Annual of the Society*, pp. 237-241. Written by James Bresnahan, this account of the group's founding, its role in planning significant parts of the programs of the annual meetings in 1977, 1978, 1980 and 1981, and its sponsorship of a special pre-meeting conference in 1979 on "Legal and Ethical Dimensions of Religious Freedom" should be consulted by those interested in its work. At the time Bresnahan wrote, he judged the task force to have been more successful in bringing people together and contributing to conversations between the two disciplines than in nurturing the publication of materials. However, Bresnahan himself, inspired perhaps by the agenda of the task force, did produce a contribution entitled "The Interaction of Religion and Law: A Post-Vatican II Roman Catholic Perspective." This was part of a larger symposium on Religion and Law published in *The Hasting Law Journal* 29 (July 1978): 1257-1660. Since Bresnahan wrote his report, plans to initiate the publication of *The Journal of Law and Religion* have come to fruition, and this will do much to make further contributions to the discussion of the relationships between these two important areas. Later, Wilson Yates and R. Kenneth Manning became co-convenors of the religion and law task force, and been followed in turn by R. Kenneth Manning and Howard S. Vogel.

Another task force, which was created in 1979 for a three-year period (subsequently extended for two more years), grew out of an interest group on ethics and economics that first met in 1978. This task force was authorized to expend up to $300 in 1979, has had a mailing list of some eighty names, and an active core group of between twenty-five and thirty persons. Jon Gunnemann was the first convenor of this group and Daniel Finn, the second.

One purpose of this task force was to exchange course syllabi, bibliographies, and papers. This was done chiefly in the first two years of the group's existence. Another purpose was to foster discussion with economists. This was achieved by having papers given at the annual meeting by guest economists such as Robert Lekachman, Harvey Segal, Jerome Kurtz and William Tabb. A third purpose of the task force was to generate papers by, and discussions among, members of the Society on matters of ethics and economics.

Papers by Warren Copeland, William Everett, Daniel Finn, Jon Gunnemann, Donald Jones, John Raines, and others have appeared on recent Society programs. (The topics of the papers by both the guest economists and the members of the Society addressing these issues are examined in chapter nine.)

From the beginning of its existence, the task force has been divided between those who wished to focus on economic policy and those who wanted to focus on business ethics. By the third year there was a consensus that the work of this group should focus on national economic policy, but this did not prevent a wide range of economic thought to be represented in the materials generated by the task force.

In 1980 a task force was established with the title "Jewish and Christian Ethics Task Force." This emerged at the time the proposal was made to change the name of the Society to include the phrase "Jewish and Christian Ethics." When the decision was made to retain the title "Christian," Franklin Sherman was asked to chair a task force on this subject as a means of responding to the concerns that were back of the movement for a name change. He asked Ronald Green to be named co-convenor.

At first the group had the idea that it should involve a significant number of Jewish scholars in the annual meetings of the Society--thus stressing the inclusiveness of the Society's interests despite the restrictiveness of its name. This idea proved more difficult to carry out than to propose. There is no recognized discipline of "Jewish ethics" that corresponds to the discipline of Christian ethics, and hence it is difficult to identify those at work in the field. The meeting schedule of the Society makes it difficult for orthodox Jews to attend, and the Society sometimes meets very far from the main locations in which Jewish scholars work. But the task force generated considerable interest in the subject, and (as will be noted in chapter ten) has prompted several papers on the programs in recent years. The task force met three years and had eight to twelve persons at its meetings. Unlike the task force on ethics and economics, which began as an interest group and became a task force, this group that began as the task force on Jewish and Christian Ethics has now become an interest group.

When the Task Force on White Racism saw its work in a larger theoretical perspective it allowed itself to be transformed into the Action Reflection Interest Group. This interest group has been concerned to examine how action and reflection interrelate in the life and work of the Christian ethicist. The first coordinator of the Action Reflection Interest Group was David Snider. The group arranged for two sessions in the 1974 program, one session in which Joseph Hough and Dan Rhoades reported on Project Understanding, a program to combat racism, and another session in which Duane K. Friesen delivered a paper on "Peace Studies: A Typology of Approaches."

In 1975 George Crowell was coordinator of the group and three items were successfully suggested for inclusion in the program. John Bennett and Gayraud Wilmore spoke from their own experience about "Social Action in the Vocation of the Social Ethicist"; Richard Taylor described "The Movement for a New Society"; and Charles Brown gave a paper on "Action Reflection as a Way of Doing Ethics."

For the 1976 meeting, Robert Breese coordinated the group. At its suggestion, two concurrent sessions were planned. Henry Clark presented a paper, "Pressure for Change: Ethical Reflection on American Life Style." Jane Cary Peck presented a paper on "Successful Social Change in School Desegregation: A Model and Case Study." The Action Reflection Group also proposed the plenary session at which Ronald Mueller, co-author of *Global Reach*, spoke on "Global Interdependence, Social Stability, and the Future of U. S. Democracy: The Dovetailing of Ethics and the Human Sciences."

For the 1977 meeting in Toronto, the group planned a tour of the city that ended in a discussion with members of the City Council over key issues in city politics. It was again being coordinated by George Crowell, who remained its leader for several subsequent years. It also arranged for John Dillon, who works with GATT-Fly, a small action organization supported by the churches of Canada and working for change in Canadian global trade policies, to address a concurrent session on "The Struggle for a More Just Trade Policy."

By 1978 the contributions of this interest group to the program of the annual meetings appeared to be declining. It helped to arrange one session, that with George A. Chauncy of the Interreligious Task Force on U. S. Food Policy. At the 1978 meeting, the group convened jointly with the Interest Group on Professional Ethicists in Non-Academic Professions, because the convenor of the latter group was not present. Out of the joint meeting came the plans for a program session in 1979 with Howard Mills and Karen Lebacqz on "Professional Ethicists in Non-Academic Roles." In 1980, Richard Snyder of the Action Reflection Group planned a Friday morning tour of the churches of New York City's upper Manhattan. The group met jointly that same year with the Human Rights Interest Group and made a number of suggestions for the 1981 meeting in Iowa. George Crowell reports that nothing came of those suggestions, nor of similar suggestions made for 1982. The year 1982, when a discouragingly small number of people attended the announced meeting, was the last year when this Interest Group functioned.

The Action Reflection Interest Group had a long and sustained period of activity. Its presence in the Society witnessed to an important issue that has been of concern to more than its own membership. In a letter, George Crowell reflects about these experiences as follows: "There are a number of reasons for [the decline in the group's role]. Participation in the group had been dwindling, and we had become less successful in getting our suggestions included in the program. On the other hand, there had been an increase in the number of items in the program with an action reflection emphasis quite apart from any initiative from us." As explained in the description of the group handed out in 1977, the purpose of the group was to balance attention paid to theological issues and selected social issues with considerations of strategy and tactics in social change. The Action Reflection Interest Group made a significant contribution to the life of the Society during the period of its activity.

Another Interest Group, on Human Rights, has been almost as active over recent years, but not as successful in getting sessions into the annual program. Its aim has been to focus the attention of the Society on human rights questions. In 1980 the program had a concurrent session on "The Inviolability Principle: Human Needs and Human Rights," convened by Richard John Neuhaus, and with a paper by the leader, George R. Lucas, Jr. At the same meeting a bibliography on the subject prepared by Lucas was made generally available to those attending. In addition to working with the Action Reflection Interest Group, the Interest Group on Human Rights has also cooperated in recent years with the Task Force on Ethics and Law.

A new Interest Group on War, Peace, Revolution and Violence was convened at the 1976 annual meeting by James Johnson and John Howard Yoder, who have since remained co-convenors. The immediate context of this action was the founding of an informal organization at the 1975 meeting of The American Academy of Religion of persons working in the broad field of ethics and violence--a group also chaired by Johnson and Yoder. It was felt that many of the people would be involved in both groups and that being associated with both parent bodies would enable them to meet twice a year to discuss their common interests.

This interest group has evolved into a regular feature of the Society's life. Meeting after the annual banquet it has frequently engaged in discussions with a variety of formats. In 1982 and 1983 the topic was the U. S. Catholic Bishops' letter on war and peace. The topic planned for 1984 was "peacemaking." Through its convenors the group has several times made suggestions for plenary topics and speakers. Growing from a membership of half-a-dozen in 1976, the group now numbers approximately fifty.

In 1977, an interest group with John Satterwhite as convenor sponsored a session on "COCU and Compensatory Justice for Minority Church Groups." Since 1980 an interest group on ethics and the Black Liberation struggle has been meeting, convened for the first three years by Charles Brown and in 1983 by Riggins Earl, Jr. Peter Paris has also been active in the leadership of this interest group.

In 1980 Thomas Shannon wrote to the executive secretary offering to convene a task force or interest group on medical ethics. This group first met in 1981. In 1983 John R. Wilcox polled members of the Society concerning the possibility of starting an interest group on Christian ethics and the professions and time will tell more about this venture. Two other interest groups have recently appeared on the programs of the Society. One is found listed under the title "Social Ethics" in the 1982 and 1983 meetings, with Richard E. Hoehn as convenor, and one, on environmental ethics, is listed in the 1983 program with David Rickett as convenor. There is also an interest group of recent origin on sexuality chaired by Robert Blaney and James B. Nelson. During 1983 William Spohn and Thomas Byrnes wrote the executive secretary about starting an interest group at the 1984 meeting on American Theological Ethics. The formation of interest groups seems to have become far more casual and more prolific than it was in earlier years of the Society's history.

A group calling itself The Working Group on Feminist Ethics was formed in 1976 and a letter sent out by Jane Cary Peck to all women listed as members of the Society at that time. The letter indicated an intention to facilitate direct contacts between women working in the field. Each person to whom the letter went was asked to furnish biographical information and data concerning professional interests and commitments and involvement in specialized theological ethical studies--primarily those related to the feminist movement. The group that has been drawn together by this process has gathered informally at Society meetings to discuss the development of feminist perspectives and methods in the field, to discuss curricular matters and share syllabi, to report on work-in-progress, and to serve as a placement network. There has been no formal membership. Women who have been interested have been asked to send a dollar to defray the costs of duplicating and distributing materials. A spin-off from these activities has been the annual Boston regional meeting of a Consultation on Ethics in Feminist Perspectives that has met each year at Andover-Newton Theological School, bringing together twenty to thirty women from the Boston, New Haven, and New York areas.

This working group has occasionally been attended by a few men. It has proven supportive of women who have been isolated in graduate school programs or in teaching positions by helping them develop feminist methodology in ethics and work on liberation content in courses and writing. The group has worked for feminist input in the programs of the Society and has been gratified as women have been nominated and elected as members of the Board of Directors and more recently to key offices in the Society. It provides a fine example of what can be accomplished when people of common interests seek to pool their information and resources. The next chapter will report on several other ways in which the members of the Society have worked among themselves and with others to further the scholarly enterprise.

4

Associations and Advocacies
The Professional Citizenship of the Society

This chapter recounts how the Society has taken its place in the wider world of professional associations. It also reports on several limited actions which the Society has taken from time to time to have an impact upon public affairs.

The Society and Other Learned Associations

In July of 1968 James Luther Adams, then president of the Society, wrote a carefully composed letter at the behest of the Board of Directors to the American Council of Learned Societies to explore the possibility that the American Society of Christians Ethics could be considered for membership in the ACLS. President Adams documented the activities of the Society with some care, enclosed the latest membership roster, stressed the accomplishments of those who made up the Society, indicated the nature and scope of its programs, and offered to supply any additional information that might be useful to the *ad hoc* committee that is, under normal circumstances, appointed to consider such a request. About two months later, the president of the ACLS, Frederick Burkhardt, responded to Adams by indicating that their Board had considered his letter and had taken no formal action, but that a clear consensus had developed that it would be "inadvisable" for the ASCE to submit an application to Council as-a-whole in a formal manner.

The stated reasons for this adverse reaction included hesitation to increase the number of constituent societies in the ACLS unless by doing so it would add substantially to the number of disciplines or to the number of individual scholars represented. The letter from Burkhardt also stated that "it was felt that the restricted range of interest of the American Society of Christian Ethics, its relative youth, and its lack of a publication medium also militated against admission."

Behind these publicly stated reasons were a number of unresolved issues in the politics of the scholarly study of religion. The ACLS was understandably concerned not to have to relate to too many separate societies in the field of religion--and it must be admitted that there were (and still are) a great many of them. The American Academy of Religion, moreover, at the time seemed to many to be an emerging kind of parent group, and representatives from it had played a central role in a conference about the relationship of the ACLS to groups concerned with the study of religion held at Princeton University just before Burkhardt's letter was sent to the president of the ASCE. Moreover, any group in the academic world dealing with the subject of religion, and more particularly one having in its name an identifiable concern for a confessional tradition, operates in such matters with a strike against it. The membership of the Society could take comfort, however, from Burkhardt's assurance that "this decision in no way reflects a judgment upon the quality or the effectiveness of the American Society of Christian Ethics as a scholarly organization, nor does lack of constituent membership in any way preclude your members from the various ACLS programs of assistance to humanistic scholarship."

While many of those having key roles in the Princeton discussions were identified with it, The American Academy of Religion, for all its phenomenal growth and remarkably diversified annual meetings, has never become the kind of overarching group that could establish contact between the several professional organizations in the study of religion and a group like the ACLS. However, near the end of the nineteen sixties another group emerged that promised to perform some of the coordinating functions between the various societies in the field of religion--functions that would need to be performed by any single body likely to qualify as a representative of all the groups concerned with the study of religion.

Word about the formation of The Council for the Study of Religion was first given to the Board of the Society at the 1970 meeting. Some preliminary explorations had been started in the fall of 1969 to determine the degree to which the Society would be interested in joining such a group. It was decided at the 1970 meeting that a liaison committee be appointed and that the Society should send an observor to the next CSR meeting to report back with a recommendation for an appropriate time for the Society to make application for membership. That time came very soon, for at the January 1971 Board meeting it was reported that the Society "had been accepted as a member of the newly formed Council on the Study of Religion." John Satterwhite was named a delegate to the new organization with a term to expire in 1973 and Max Stackhouse to a term to expire in 1972. The Society agreed to make a contribution of fifty cents per member for *The Bulletin* and seventy-five cents per member for the general budget. It also assumed the travel expenses of its delegates to the CSR meetings. The 1972 Board meeting received a report from delegate Stackhouse about the work of the new group. Stackhouse detailed its efforts to support publication and scholarship, its plans to make a directory of undergraduate departments of religion, its role in planning the 1972 International Congress on the Study of Religion, and the possibility it would be setting up a computerized administrative office to handle routine things (like dues billing for member societies). The Board struggled with whether or not the benefits to be derived warranted the sizeable financial commitment entailed. It was pointed out that larger organizations, like the American Academy of Religion and the Society of Biblical Literature, would probably benefit more from the services of such an office than the much smaller ASCE. (Ironically, time would see the two larger groups cease to use the central services of the Council, and the ASCE continue to use them, not only for dues collection purposes, but for printing *The Selected Papers* and *The Annual*. Douglas Sturm was named to be a delegate and became the third person to represent the Society in this way. In future years delegates to the Council would include Edward Long, Jr. (calendar years 1973-75), Glen Stassen (1976-78), and Peter Paris (1979-1984), as well as the executive secretaries serving *ex officio* during their terms of office. Douglas Sturm also served as a delegate 1973-74 and 1975-77 and rendered especially important service to the CSR. He was elected its vice-chairman in 1975 and thereafter became its chairman for a term.

The Council for the Study of Religion proposed to hold a conference in Washington bringing together all of its member societies. This was first proposed for September of 1973 and the Board authorized the Society to participate to the extent of planning and conducting one or two plenary sessions, but was not willing to change the date of its annual meeting to coincide with this contemplated larger meeting. The meeting subsequently was rescheduled for October of 1974 as a joint meeting of the AAR/SBL/SSSR.

In the report on the work of the CSR given to the 1974 meeting of the Board the creation of TOIL (Teaching Opportunities Inventory Listing) was announced and the service charge of $25.00 yearly to participating institutions made known. It was also reported that the CSR had been appointed to administer travel grants, in amounts of $250-$600, made available from the ACLS. Across the subsequent years the CSR has undertaken other projects, including cooperation with The Women's Caucus on Religious Studies in the development of affirmative action programs, efforts to stimulate the establishment of religious studies programs in community colleges, and the initiation and launching of *The Religious Studies Review*.

While the financial costs of membership in the Council have been high they have provided two distinct benefits. On the one hand, membership in the CSR has made an enormous difference in the administrative work of our executive secretary. The burden of sending out dues notices, keeping the roster up-to-date, and attending to the production arrangements involved in publishing *The Annual* would be unbearable without the help afforded by the CSR. On the other hand, the support of the CSR helps to advance the cause of scholarship in the field of religion in ways that the Society would not be able to do acting by itself.

In the early 1970s a number of groups involved in the scholarly study of religion decided to hold an International Congress of Learned Societies in the Field of Religion, in Los Angeles, California, September 1-5, 1972. The Board of Directors began to plan the Society's participation in this gathering at the 1970 meeting, when an invitation was reported to it by the executive secretary. The invitation, which came through Joseph Hough on behalf of a committee headed by James Robinson, called for moving our annual meeting to coincide with the dates of the Congress, as many other groups were doing. The invitation was discussed at length, with particular attention devoted to the purpose of the Congress, whether it would fulfill the purpose of the annual meeting of the Society, and to what extent membership in the ASCE overlapped the membership in other societies involved. Following this discussion the Board decided respectfully to decline to hold either its 1972 or 1973 annual meeting in conjunction with the International Congress, but indicated that it would encourage its members to attend. It also empowered the Executive Committee to see if arrangements could be made for the Society to participate in the Congress in some other ways, such as participating in the general planning of the Congress, holding some special meeting, or co-sponsoring a session with the *Societas Ethica*. Negotiations were undertaken and at the 1972 Board meeting the vice-president reported that the Society had been asked to sponsor a Saturday session fron 10:30 a.m to noon, and that planning for other events had begun in consultation with the chairperson of the ethics section of the AAR. When the vice-president, along with other members of the Society who were in attendance at the planning sessions of the Congress in Atlanta in the fall of 1971, learned that the Society would have responsibility for this Saturday session, a consensus developed that Douglas Sturm should be invited to deliver the address as a representative of the Society. Agreement to invite him to do this was made, without Sturm's knowledge, through mail ballot, and the invitation extended to him as a surprise and as a token of appreciation for the many things he had done for the Society and the high esteem in which its members view his scholarship.

Incumbent president Long, who planned to attend, agreed to preside at the session at which Professor Sturm spoke on "Corporations, Constitutions, and Covenants: A Study of Forms of Human Relations and the Problem of Legitimacy." Sturm's address was subsequently published in *The Journal of the American Academy of Religion* XLI (September 1973): 331-354.

The meeting in Los Angeles was valuable in several other ways. Docent Harry Aronson, of Lund, Sweden, the secretary of *Societas Ethica*, attended the Congress with other several other colleagues to introduce their Society to the States and contacts between European and American ethicists were made that have had all too few counterparts across the years. The Society has tried a number of times to initiate better contacts with the *Societas Ethica* with letters of cordial greetings, with encouragement of its members to attend the European meetings whenever possible, and with an occasional distribution of the membership list of our European colleagues in the mailings to our members. But it cannot be claimed that we have kept the relationships between the two Societies as functional and as productive as might have been the case.

At the Los Angeles meeting the president of the Society was also asked to preside at a general morning session of the Congress, and to introduce Professor Dorothy Sölle of Cologne, Germany, who spoke on "Political Theology and the Liberation of Man."

The session at which Sturm spoke also entertained and passed, with but one dissenting vote, a motion proposed by John C. Bennett, a former president of the Society, calling for the following action: (1) that a committee be appointed by the presiding chairman to draft a resolution expressing moral disgust over the dehumanization of man as perpetuated by the continued and expanded bombing of North Vietnam, and (2) that the text of such a statement be transmitted to the Program Steering Committee of the Congress with the request that some means be found, possibly at some plenary meeting of the Congress, to allow it to endorse such a statement. The statement, as prepared by the committee (which consisted of John C. Bennett, Victor Obenhaus, and William Byron) was drawn up as follows, and sent with the resolution:

> The International Congress of the Learned Societies in the Field of Religion, organized around the theme of "Religion and the Humanizing of Man" wishes to reaffirm the value of Human-life-as-such in Indochina. Moreover, we urge the American people to comprehend and ponder the human consequences of the fact that today in their name, land and cultures in Southeast Asia are being subjected to continuous and disproportional destruction.
>
> As we invite all Americans to reject on religious and moral grounds the slaughter in Southeast Asia, we urge them as well to press upon their national government the moral necessity of ending it now. This statement was transmitted to the leadership of the Congress with the urgent request that adequate opportunity be given for the Congress or its membership to indicate their support and agreement.

It is difficult to be precise about the relationship between the ASCE and the ethics section of the AAR. Many members of the Society are active participants and even officers in the AAR group. Through them the interchange between the program activities of the two groups has been very evident. But the Society has done very little as an organization to relate to the AAR except as this relationship is entailed through the activities of the CSR. In a similar fashion the Society has been more than willing to have the Society for Values in Higher Education hold gatherings in conjunction with its annual meeting, but has not joined with the SVHE in any program planning or joint activity.

At the annual meeting in 1974, a floor-introduced motion was passed which instructed the Board of Directors to investigate during the succeeding year the advisability of periodically holding the annual meeting of the Society simultaneously with the annual meetings of other related societies. A study of overlapping memberships showed that 241 out of 527 members of the ASCE were also members of AAR, and it was argued that having meetings together would help to save money on travel expenses and also increase the interaction between the Society and other groups. The membership of the Society was polled by mail to ascertain whether it thought that such an arrangement would be helpful. Only eleven responses came back. After considerable discussion, the Board, by a vote of 13 to 1, decided to recommend to the annual meeting in 1975 that the Society continue to meet separately. Efforts from the floor to propose an alternative that involved meeting with another group every third year were defeated by a margin of nearly 5 to 1, and the meeting pattern has remained unchanged ever since.

The Society has also engaged over the years in conversations with representatives from different organizations exploring possibilities of cooperation. For instance, in 1963 there were discussions between the executive committee of the Board of Directors and the Executive Director of the Aspen Institute for Humanistic Studies exploring whether the Society could have a role in the development of a theological section of the Institute. The next year Paul Ramsey, who had been instrumental in opening up the initial conversations, reported that the prospect of establishing such a center looked dim. Nothing further seems to have come of this matter.

In 1971, upon the fiftieth anniversary of the American Civil Liberties Union, the Board sent greetings to that organization. One of the most recent actions of the Society in cooperating with various other professional organizations was a decision in 1983 to support the National Humanities Alliance with a per capita apportionment of eighteen cents. The Alliance is a coalition of some forty learned societies, libraries, and educational institutions which present their interests to the Congress and governmental agencies. The Society undoubtedly will continue to find ways of being a good member of the community of learned societies.

Good Causes and Public Stands

The Society has been primarily devoted to the nurture of scholarship and to the cultivation of collegiality among those persons who are professionally concerned with Christian ethics. But from time-to-time it has expressed itself on a social, moral, or public policy matter about which some of its members have been sufficiently concerned to press for action. There has been no regular pattern to the appearance of such statements and they have been handled in a variety of ways. The work of the task forces on white racism, conspiracy trials, and the celebration of the nation's bicentennial, that has been described in the previous chapter, also should be considered as part of this overall genre of the Society's work in dealing with public questions.

Apart from the work of the task forces mentioned, the first action of the Board that comes under this category was taken at the 1968 meeting, when the Board recommended that the Society endorse the 1940 Statement on Academic Freedom of the American Association of University Professors. At the same meeting the Board instructed the president to write to the AAUP requesting that consideration be given to the formulation of standards of institutional responsibility in cases of the disability of faculty members. It also asked the president to inquire of the American Association of Theological Schools just how academic freedom was to be understood in relationship to the professed religious aims of certain types of educational institution.

In 1969, the annual business meeting considered a resolution presented by Preston Williams "urging that all small, informal theological discussion groups throughout the nation open their groups to participation by Black churchmen." The implication of this motion was to urge members to press for such inclusion in groups to which they belonged. After vigorous discussion the motion was amended to include persons of other ethnic groups and was unanimously adopted.

The following year James Luther Adams raised in the Board meeting the possibility that the members of the Society should be concerned about the investment portfolios of the churches and theological schools with which they are associated, and urged that the Society consider ways to communicate about this issue to students and teachers in various institutions. No specific action was taken by the Board, although Frederick Carney suggested that the program committee might include a session on the matter in the program of the next annual meeting (which it did not do).

The 1971 Board also received a letter from Elizabeth Johns to John Satterwhite expressing concern over the status of women in the profession of Christian ethics and in the membership of the ASCE. The Board suggested that the matter should be given attention in the program for the following year. The program in 1972 did hear a paper on women's liberation but not one that specifically addressed the concerns of Elizabeth John's letter.

Six years later another resolution addressing a public policy matter was presented to the Society for adoption. A motion, proposed by the Board and adopted by the membership by acclamation, declared "It is the sense of the ASCE that the anniversary of Martin Luther King's birthday be appropriately recognized as a national holiday in the United States."

In 1980, another matter of great concern was considered by the Society. The subject for this action arose in the Saturday afternnon business meeting, which passed a resolution in principle, leaving the final wording to be determined by the incoming Board at its Sunday morning session. The resolution expressed deep concern over the Vatican declaration against Hans Küng and its investigation of Edward Schillebeeckx and other Catholic scholars. It continued, "We acknowledge the concern of church authorities for the integrity of teaching in a pastoral setting. Nonetheless, we insist that to suppress creative and critical theological inquiry discourages theological scholarship within the church and has a chilling effect on the theological exploration necessary for the successful continuation of the ecumenical dialogue. Furthermore, to restrict creative and critical theological inquiry without following the requirements of due process offends against academic freedom, justice, and human rights." Another motion passed by the Society instructed that the previous motion be distributed to Pope John Paul II, Archbishop Jean Jadot (the apostolic delegate to the United States), the Sacred Congregation for the Doctrine of the Faith at Vatican City, and to the press, e.g. through Religious News Service and National Catholic News Service.

At the meeting in 1981 Nancy Bancroft offered a resolution noting the resurgence of militant racism in the country's life. It noted that racist groups derive support for their propaganda from questionable scientific and academic works, some claiming a genetic basis for racial inferiority, and it declared that such special theories fuel and legitimate the activity of racist organizations. The resolution called upon all persons to condemn and counter racist activity and organizations, to scrutinize the propaganda and questionable academic literature upon which racism depends, and to renew both verbal and practical commitment to racial equality. The executive secretary was directed to circulate this statement to all Society members and to publish it in several places. He was also instructed to urge public officials to resist efforts to erode the principle of human rights. The Bancroft resolution, rather extensive in its scope and implications, solicited a floor dicussion of some length and it was referred to a committee to report a revised version at an adjourned business session on Sunday morning. The revised version passed without difficulty.

Disturbed by the timing and logistics rather than the substance of both the Küng and the racism resolutions, the Board subsequently undertook to adopt a policy regarding the introduction of resolutions. It hoped to avoid the hassles that are created when the business meeting must be adjourned to Sunday morning in order to handle such matters. After considering the problem, even to the point of thinking about adopting bylaws strictly determining procedures, the Board settled for an informal notice to the members asking that they submit any proposed resolution for consideration by the annual meeting to the president of the Society as early as possible, preferably no later than the end of the first plenary session. The president is then, after consultation with the Executive Committee, to name an *ad hoc* committee which can bring a report to the annual business meeting, suggesting adoption or rejection. The *ad hoc* committee also has the power to redraft the text. This informal understanding also has within it a declaration of general policy which reads: "The formulation and publication of resolutions on issues of the day is not among the purposes of the Society stated in its Constitution and Bylaws. Occasionally however, issues arise that are especially pertinent to the Society's purpose. The Society needs to deliberate such resolutions with care but without disrupting the annual business meeting and the other activites of the annual meeting."

In 1982 it was learned that the National 4-H Center had denied the use of its facilities to the New Ways ministry. President Daniel Maguire was asked to make inquiry into the accuracy of this information and the reasons behind it. The New Ways Ministry provides a ministry of reconciliation and social justice for Catholic gay and lesbian persons and other sexual minorities. The investigation revealed that the 4-H Council had also refused the use of its facilities to such groups as Amnesty International, the Interreligious Task Forces on U.S. Food Policy, and the Religious Task Force for El Salvador. This information was reported in a memorandum to the members of the Society for their information and at its 1983 meeting the Board adopted a resolution that the Society will "not meet at the 4-H Center in the foreseeable future because of unanswered questions regarding that institution's respect for the rights of all persons."

This record of actions would hardly suggest the Society has become an advocacy or action group rather than a learned society. There is almost nothing here that constitutes the kind of political activity that would alter the tax status of the Society or commit its membership to a major partisan agenda. The actions taken by the Society witness in most cases to a high regard for the fundamental amenities of scholarship and a concern to protect the right of persons to pursue the truth without interference from external authorities or distortions from arbitrary pressures.

It takes an enormous amount of time and effort from many individuals to sustain the ongoing life of even a modestly complex organization such as the Society. Almost all of that effort is done voluntarily and even the executive secretaries, who carry the pivotal responsibility for keeping all things functioning smoothly, though paid a modest honorarium, contribute far beyond the call of duty. The activities that have been described in this section are crucial for making possible the interchange of ideas that occurs about the discipline through the programs of the Society. We will now look at the substantive content of the Society's work by examining the issues it has canvassed in the papers and panels that have constituted the programs at the annual meetings.

Part Three
Substance

5

Foundational Issues on the Programs

The third part of this history is concerned with the deliberations of the Society on the substantive issues of Christian ethics. The focus is still upon the Society as a professional group. All of the materials reported upon here and in the next several chapters were first presented as papers (or in panel discussions) at the annual meetings of the Society.

The programs of the Society have been a fertile seedbed of Christian ethical reflection in the past quarter-century. The substance of the papers and sessions has found its way into the main stream of the discipline. Sometimes this is obvious, as in the plenary sessions at which members of the Society have been asked to share ideas stemming from nearly finished but not yet published books. It was on this basis that Paul Lehmann discussed *The Transfiguration of Politics* at the 1974 meeting and James Gustafson, *Ethics in a Theocentric Perspective, Volume Two*, at the 1983 meeting. In other cases, scholars from both inside and outside of the Society have tried out ideas at its annual meetings they would later incorporate into books or articles. But papers and panels are not always trial balloons with which an author explores a topic before putting it into published form. They are sometimes condensed and truncated versions of themes already explored more fully elsewhere. They are frequently examinations of special matters that would not warrant treatment in a monograph. Panels bring together several scholars to share points of view. It is much easier to pull together a panel for a program than to put together a symposium in a book, and legitimate to do so on a less comprehensive basis.

Even if the account in this part of our history does not tell the whole story of Christian ethical reflection since 1959, it does shed light upon the extent to which particular topics have been of concern to an important group of scholarly ethicists. Such a catalogue of topics covered tells us something that is quite important, even though it is slightly different from an examination of how issues relate to each other in a systematic way. In telling the story of the Society's deliberations we are faced with about four hundred presentations in the form of either papers or panels. It is valuable to observe the groupings into which such a large number of presentations fall when examined for their content and focus of concern. In order to handle the great number and complexity of materials we have devised rubrics for grouping the topics. Such rubrics have nothing immutable or final about them, and a number of the papers may be placed in more than one classification. Not even the Society of Christian Ethics has been able to keep the parameters of analytical categories clean cut, or see to it that the work of individuals conforms strictly to predefined agendas. Another account might very well sort out the topics differently. Moreover, to cover such a body of materials for the historical purposes of this account makes it necessary to give something that is more akin to a restaurant menu than to a book of recipes. Menus concentrate attention on what has been served, rather than upon how each dish has been prepared. They tell about the establishment more than about the ingredients in each dish. Even so, menus are valuable clues to the nature of establishments and the kinds of things with which they deal, as well as to the eating preferences of certain groups.

Over the years, the largest number of subjects appearing on the programs has fallen under the rubric "foundational issues." This term covers sessions that have been primarily concerned with the biblical, historical, philosophical, theological and social-scientific grounds for the doing of Christian ethics. While this group of papers is almost twice as large as any other single category, it still constitutes only about one-third of the total program content of the meetings. The discussion of theoretical issues by themselves has not been the chief preoccupation of the Society, but it must be borne in mind that papers addressing specific issues and problems often have a theoretical component as important as that of the papers discussed in this chapter.

Biblical Foundation of Christian Ethics

The first two discussions of the role of the Bible in ethical reflection were made before the Society by invited guests. Paul W. Meyer of the Colgate Rochester Divinity School addressed the Society in 1965 on "Some Considerations on the Role of Exegesis in Ethical Reflection." His paper was mimeographed and distributed to the membership. John L. McKenzie followed the next year with "Personal Dignity and

Personal Responsibility in the New Testament." (McKenzie's paper was not distributed and is not in the records.) Meyer noted the two biblicisms which H. Richard Niebuhr rejected in *The Responsible Self*. He suggested that the most reliable exegesis of biblical materials depends upon putting the text into its historical setting and understanding it in light of its theological meaning. He illustrated his method by looking at I Corinthians 15, examining how a number of theological commentators have interpreted it, and proposing his own exegesis.

Seventeen years later, another guest spoke to the Society on the role of the Bible in ethical reflection. This presentation was also given at a plenary session. By now the terminology was hermeneutics rather than exegesis, and the relevant literature was more extensive. In "Discipleship and Patriarchy: Early Christian Ethos and Christian Ethics in a Feminist Theological Perspective," Elisabeth Schüssler Fiorenza of Notre Dame University placed the emphasis on the role of the church as a community of moral discourse. "The moral authority of the Bible," declared Professor Schüssler Fiorenza, "is grounded in a community that is capable of sustaining scriptural authority in faithful remembrance, liturgical celebration, ecclesial governance and continual reinterpretation of its own biblical roots and traditions." This process is not without difficulties and miscarriages, as the paper showed by recounting how the Bible has been used in repressive as well as in emancipating ways. The argument also suggested that the biblical traditions, adequately interpreted through the joint efforts of biblical scholars and Christian ethicists, can be a helpful contribution to feminist liberation theology. This paper is published in *The 1982 Annual* together with the responses given by Bruce Birch and Thomas Ogletree. Professor Schüssler Fiorenza published shortly thereafter an article entitled "Feminist Theology and New Testament Interpretation," *The Journal for the Study of the Old Testament* XXII (1982): 32-46.

In the intervening years nearly a dozen members of the Society have examined these and similar issues. In 1973 Carl E. Braaten argued in a paper entitled "Eschatological Ethics: Toward a Theory of Christian Ethics," that while the roots of Christian ethics belong in biblical eschatology, few contemporary ethicists acknowledge this and many of them completely ignore it. All members received this paper in mimeographed form. Braaten rooted his eschatological starting point for ethics in the kingdom of God preached by Jesus and showed how this idea can be reciprocally related to philosophical ethics to produce a more adequate view of the Christian life than was available when first enunciated by

Jesus. In 1983 Thomas Ogletree, himself about ready to publish a book, *The Use of the Bible in Christian Ethics* (Fortress, 1983), returned to the theme with a paper, "The Eschatological Horizon of New Testament Social Thought," in which he delineated how the social radicalism and institutional creativity which are found in the New Testament can contribute to original thinking about social matters.

In 1976 Larry Rasmussen and Bruce Birch presented a session on "The Role of the Bible in Christian Ethics." They shortly thereafter published *The Bible and Ethics in the Christian Life* (Augsburg, 1976). In 1978 Stephen Charles Mott presented "Equalitation Aspects of the Biblical Theory of Justice." In this paper, as in his subsequent book, *Biblical Ethics and Social Change* (Oxford, 1982), Mott argued against those views of justice that contrast it sharply with love and grace. Biblical justice, in Mott's view, is a creating rather than a preserving justice, and is therefore actively concerned for the protection of the weak and the afflicted. Karen Lebacqz contributed a paper in 1983 which examined the use of biblical parables, particularly the parable of the laborers in the vineyard found in Matthew 20:1-16, as sources of ethical insight on "Justice, Economics, and the Uncomfortable Kingdom." Her conclusion was that "justice requires redress of imbalance, not simply distribution on the basis of merit."

Raymond Anderson, in a paper at the 1979 annual meeting entitled "The Minimal Ethic Phenomena in the Gospels," examined the contention current among a number of biblical scholars that the content of ethical teaching in the Gospels is relatively meager. Examining the Gospel of Mark and the Gospel of John he showed how strong were the tendencies in the early church against burdening the free and responsive life of the new convenantal people with too great an ethic. The same year Allen Verhey examined "The Use of Scripture in Moral Argument: Methodological Reflection on Walter Rauschenbusch." Verhey examined the way in which appeals to scripture in moral argument are always authorization-using arguments, of which three played a role in Rauschenbusch's thought. He also suggested that scripture cannot function authoritatively apart from tradition, community, reason, and experience. Hence, the use of scripture by Christian ethicists must remain constantly open to the criticism that comes from the Christian community and even from the scripture itself.

In 1980, George L. Frear, Jr. considered "Universalization and Biblical Particularities." He took issue with Barth's contention that the moral command is always special to each person and occasion. Frear argued that universalizing--that is, developing judgments about right and wrong that are the same under similar circumstances and speaking about obligation in general terms--is central to moral reasoning. He showed how this process can make use of biblical materials. The next year, William M. Longsworth developed a systematic account of the ethical perspective of Saint Paul. He looked at the entire Pauline corpus and showed that Paul gave more shape to a normative conception of the Christian life than has been commonly acknowledged and that Paul's method of moral reasoning operated throughout all the particular judgments that he made. This paper is published in *The Annual.* In 1983 Edward H. Schroeder discussed "Mosaic and Christic Ethos in the Gospel of John" indicating that though the Fourth Gospel contains no ethical teaching of the type found in the synoptics or in Paul--no Sermon on the Mount, no *Haustateln*, no references to the decalogue, et. al., it does shed light on matters of ethical import by showing that the human ethos becomes changed in a new world of grace and truth.

Historical Studies, the Uses of History and Cultural Diagnoses

The group of papers dealing with historical materials or the nature of history is three times as large as the group of papers dealing with the use of the Bible in ethical reflection, but both groups of papers have some of the same disparate qualities.

About half the historically oriented papers have been studies of particular figures, movements, or periods of the history of Christian ethics. Below is a list of papers, in the years given, that come under this category. Of this group only four (marked below with an asterisk) were distributed to members, though a number were published, as will be indicated in the paragraph that follows the list.

1962 Donovan Smucker, "The Permanent and the Transient Elements in the Social Gospel"
1962 Arthur C. Cochrane, "Natural Law in John Calvin"
1964 Frederick S. Carney, "The Fifteenth Century Background of Reformation Ethics"
1966 Theodore W. Olsen, "American Social Theory and Theology: Holism and Particularism"*
1969 C. C. Goen, "The Intellectual History of 18th Century American as Rewritten by Alan Heimart"
1972 Roger L. Shinn, "Reinhold Niebuhr's Criticism of Utopianism: A Reassessment"*
1974 Max Myers, "Classical Liberalism and Hegel's Concept of Freedom"
1974 Richard L. Spencer, "Hegel and Moltmann: The Dialectic of Need and the Dialectic of Hope"

1978 Theodore W. Olsen, "Millenial Ethics and the Holy Community"
1978 Ernest Best, "Ethics in a Whiteheadian Context"
1978 George W. Forell, "Christ Against Culture: The Political Ethics of Tertullian"*
1979 Dennis McCann, "Ernst Troeltsch's Political Ethics"
1978 Edmund Leites, "Conscience, Morality and Human Rights in Locke and the Levellers"
1981 George W. Forell, "The Ethics of Early Christian Monasticism: Symbol and Reality"*
1981 David Trickett, "Jonathan Edwards and an Ethics of Universal Responsibility"
1981 Philip J. Rossi, "Autonomy and Community: A Kantian Foundation for Moral Theology"
1982 Timothy F. Sedgwick, "F. D. Maurice and Anglican Social Thought"

(The number of papers from this list that were published, or prompted publications on related material by their authors, is fairly significant. C. C. Goen's paper was published in *The Journal of the Liberal Ministry* IX [Fall 1969] 24-31. Roger Shinn's, as "Realism, Radicalism, and Eschatology in Reinhold Niebuhr: A Reassessment," *The Journal of Religion* 52 (October 1974): 409-423. A related article by Dennis McCann appeared under the title "Socialism--Ernst Troeltsch," in *The Journal of Religion Ethics* IV [Spring 1976]: 159-180. Edmund Leites published "Conscience, Leisure, and Learning: Locke and Levellers," in *Sociological Analysis XXXIX [Spring 1978]: 36-61. Part of Philip Rossi's material is incorporated in Together Toward Hope: A Journey to Moral Theology* [Notre Dame, 1983] and George Forell's, in *A History of Christian Ethics*, Volume One [Augsburg, 1979]).

None of these papers was sought as a contribution by a guest scholar, as were three of the papers dealing with biblical materials. Very few members of the Society would deny the importance of remaining abreast of the history of Christian ethics. But a graduate student preparing for comprehensives would probably find the programs of the Society an insufficient source of materials with which to prepare, and the materials distributed to the members a still less adequate resource.

The members of the Society have not been uninterested in history--particularly recent history. One of the most popular Sunday morning plenaries was a panel devised in 1977 at which three elder statespersons in the field were to reminisce about the developments which they had seen take place in the period from the 1930s to the 1970s. One of them, John Bennett, had to withdraw because his wife was ill, so the sessions consisted of presentations by James Luther Adams and Walter G. Muelder. Each spoke autobiographically, to the delight and edification of those attending. Muelder has left a manuscript of his remarks, which end with an eloquent plea for taking cultural wholes and global interdependence seriously.

In 1964, James Gustafson gave a paper entitled "Direction from the Past: An Essay in favor of Christianity in 'Post Christian' Ethics." In 1969 Jan M. Lochman gave a guest paper on "The Significance of Historical Events for Ethical Decision." Lochman was that year the Fosdick Visiting Professor at Union Theological Seminary in New York. Interest in his presentation was heightened by the speaker's well-known efforts to maintain Christian integrity in a Marxist setting.

Two papers from the 1978 meeting, both readily available in printed volumes, addressed the fundamental question as to how historical data and knowledge are useful for doing ethics. James T. Johnson's paper, "The Uses of History for Religious Ethics," has been published in *The Journal of Religious Ethics* 7 (1979): 97-115. Waldo Beach's presidential address, "The Old and the New in Christian Ethics," is found in the 1978 edition of *The Selected Papers*. Beach examined the tremendous conceptual changes--or "major revolutions" as he called them--that have affected our view of reality. These consist of a new cosmology, the loss of a vivid sense of a continuing individual destiny, belief in the power of citizens to determine the social and governmental structures under which they live, the Marxist awareness of how much economic institutions determine social norms, and the rise of technology. Beach argued that in face of these changes three abiding affirmations of Christian faith remain: trust in a transcendent beneficent divine will, the belief that the sources of moral good and evil rest on voluntaristic foundations, and the contention that the norm of *agape*, as exemplified in the person of Christ, remains the abiding standard of Christian behavior.

A third group of papers dealing with historical matters may be characterized most succinctly by the phrase "diagnoses of culture." These papers try to read the nature of the milieu in which we live and think. Robert Lee had the first paper which can be classified in this group. In 1964 he read "The Problem and Meaning of Leisure in America," portions of which appeared in *Religion and Leisure in America* (Abingdon, 1964). Two years later Harvey Cox shared "Second Thoughts on the Secular Society." In 1972 Gibson Winter gave a paper at the opening plenary session on "Foundation of Ethos: Social Ethics in an Era of Cultural Transformation." Franklin Sherman and John Giles Milhaven responded to this paper. Winter's paper analyzed the historical cultural situation in which the human sciences do their work. It identified the basic informing motifs of our age as the recovery of earth, the notion of society, and the centrality of *praxis*. A crisis develops when these are subverted. Some of the themes later to appear in Winter's book, *Liberating Creation* (Crossroads, 1981), are evident in the 1972 paper, but they undergo considerable refinement in the intervening years. (Gibson's paper may be equally germane to the discussion of societal and social scientific matters that are looked at in the last section of this chapter.) In a paper delivered at the 1976 meeting under the title, "Roots of the American Revolutionary Tradition: A Critical Analysis," John M. Gessell argued that the concept of liberty that motivated the American revolution has been largely lost to the general American consciousness of the present and that liberation thinkers provide the most promising opportunity for recapturing its essential dynamic in the social order.

Individualism has twice been the topic of analysis. In 1978 Eric Mount gave a paper, "The Pitfalls and Possibilities of American Individualism." This has been published in a revised form in *The Review of Religious Research* 22 (June 1981): 362-376. Robin Lovin's paper "Empiricism and Christian Social Thought: The Epistemology of Individualism," was printed in *The 1982 Annual*. The Presidential Address of 1980 by Donald Shriver, which appeared in the March 26, 1980 issue of *The Christian Century* even before it was released in the Society's *Selected Papers*, was on "The Pain and Promise of Pluralism." Shriver showed that the rationalism associated with a liberal (and essentially Protestant) America wrongly presumed to be universalistic, and he offered certain suggestions for responding to the loss of its influence. He urged theological ethicists to maintain intellectual comradeship with the physical, biological, and social scientists who are engaged in a search for the scope and limits of the human. He upheld the importance of cultivating empathy and the art of forgiveness in politics. In this paper we can see the beginnings of a break with the tendency of Christian realism to portray political life too harshly--a break that has since become increasingly evident in Shriver's thinking.

Christian Ethics and Philosophical Understanding

The members of the Society of Christian Ethics have seldom been unaware that moral philosophy is an important aspect of ethical reflection--though they cannot be accused of having focused attention on any one way of doing philosophy, be it existentially or analytically. The interest in philosophy, while not dominant in the programs, has at times been given unique visibility. In two instances, philosophers whose thinking has been of particular interest to Christian ethicists have been invited as guests of the Society and to engage in a discussion of their work in a plenary session on Sunday morning. The first of these occurred in 1973, when Hannah Arendt responded to papers on her thought prepared by William W. Everett and Roland Delattre. Two years later, William Frankena of the University of Michigan was present to converse with Stanley Hauerwas and Frederick Carney.

While having philosphers present in person to respond to discussions of their own work has been unusual, it has not been unusual to have papers dealing with the thought of moral philosophers. The thinking of John Rawls on justice has been considered in two papers. In 1974 Wayne Proudfoot offered "A Theological Critique of Rawls' Theory of Justice." A version of his paper was published under the title "Rawls on the Individual and the Social" in *The Journal of Religious Ethics* II (Fall 1974): 107-128. Three years later Merle Longwood and Henry Clark gave a joint session entitled "Two Critiques of the Ethics of John Rawls." A paper on Polanyi scheduled for 1982 had to be cancelled.

The greatest number of papers dealing with the thought or the influence of a particular philosopher have been the ones about Karl Marx and his influence. The thinking of Marx has undoubtedly been taken into account in sessions dealing with both economic matters and East-West relationships, but the relationship of Marxism to Christianity has been a subject of frequent inquiry and has been on the following programs of the Society in a quite wide range of treatments.

1968 Jürgen Moltmann (with James Luther Admas and Dan D. Rhoades responding), "Freedom in Christian and Marxist Perspective"

1972 Thomas Ogletree, "Ideology and Ethical Reflection"

1973 Marx W. Wartofsky (a guest from Boston University) "The Present State of Marxist Ethics"

1978 James Will, "The Principles of Concretion in Marxist and Christian Ethics"

1980 Nancy Bancroft, "Does Marx Have an Ethical Theory?"

1981 Paul Peachey, "Individual Personality in Soviet Social Theory"

1983 Ruth L. Smith, "The Individual and Society in Reinhold Niebuhr and Karl Marx"

(The paper by James Will, entitled "Christian-Marxist Ethical Dialogue from a Process Perspective," was published in *Encounter* 42 [Autumn 1981]: 353-367. The paper given by Jürgen Moltmann was published in a revised form in Thomas Ogletree, ed., *Openings for Marxist Christian Dialogue* [Abingdon, 1969]. The paper by Nancy Bancroft was published in *Soundings* LXIII [Summer 1980]: 214-229).

In addition to the papers listed, a presentation by Raymond L. Whitehead was given at the 1983 meeting on "Ethics in Post-Mao China: Modernization and Humanization." His paper is pertinent to this topic but approaches the issues he discusses more through social analysis than philosophical inquiry.

One of the subjects that has received probing treatment in the programs of the Society has been the nature of justice. Two presidential addresses have been devoted to this issue. In 1965 Prentiss L. Pemberton spoke on "Concerning the Historical Problem of Knowledge About Justice." Pemberton was concerned with how ethicists and students of social processes may discern early enough the misdirections that cause enormous subsequent changes in a society, and more particularly the consequences that are likely to ensue because America has never sufficiently clarified her ideals of justice and freedom. Delving into the biblical and historical backgrounds of an adequate view of justice, Pemberton showed the ambivalence and uncertainty in modern liberalism about this matter and suggested the need for the United States to put its conceptual understanding in order if it is to deal with the problems of the future.

In 1981, Douglas Sturm, speaking on "The Prism of Justice: *E Pluribus Unum?*," was pursuing a similar theme. Noting that the Word of God involves a demand for political justice, Sturm suggested that thinking about justice requires several strands, not dissimilar to the bands of light refracted by a prism. The four strands, together with representative advocates, identified by Sturm are: justice as liberty (Nozick and Flathman); justice as equality (Honore and Rawls); justice as community (Gould and Johann); and justice as wisdom (Strauss and Voegelin). Sturm argued that the principles of liberty and quality are centrifugal in character and must be balanced by principles of community and wisdom which are centripetal in their effect. Sturm's address achieved the distinction of eliciting a subsequent paper by another member in which Sturm's scheme was amplified and extended to apply to thinking about economics as well as to contemporary politics. Warren Copeland's topic in 1983 was "The Economic Policy Debate and Sturm's 'Prism of Justice'."

Other papers on the programs dealing with justice in

philosophical terms have been Merle Longwood's "Compensatory Justice: A New Mode of Social Response" (1971) and Drew Christiansen's "On Relative Equality" (originally planned for 1983 but postponed to 1984).

The nature of moral reasoning has also been examined a number of different ways in papers given at the Society's meetings. In 1974 Frederick Carney presented a paper "On the Nature of Moral Argument." In 1974 Donald Evans considered "Christian Ethics and Linguistic Analysis." The presidential address of James Luther Adams in 1969 was entitled "The Pragmatic Theory of Meaning: One Approach to Method in Christian Ethics." Adams traced this theory back to Charles S. Peirce, showed how much it stresses consequential rather than metaphysical measures of adequacy, and brought the discussion into contemporary times by noting ways in which the thought of both Nowell-Smith and Braithwaite is colored by similar assumptions. Adams then chided the pragmatists for being too individualistic, thus neglecting social consequences, and set down certain principles that he contended must be kept in mind if Christian ethicists are to embrace the pragmatic theory of meaning without introducing distortions into the doing of ethics. In conclusion, Adams reminded the members of the Society that the consequences of belief depend very heavily upon the distributions of power that are at work in any historical situation and that no one configuration of power is to be so trusted as to exempt it from religious criticism.

While he did not use the terminology, Edward L. Long, Jr. in his presidential address in 1973 developed a pragmatic view of the authority of the Christian ethicist. Concerned with "Christian Ethics and the Problem of Credibility," he considered the ways in which the work of the ethicist commends itself. Suggesting that appeals to external sponsorship have lost their power, that the use of reason no longer produces a consensus, and that identification with a special group or tradition no longer authenticates commitments outside of the convictional circle involved, his treatment argued that the credibility of the ethicist is grounded in competency rather than correctness, in comprehensive adequacy rather than in unquestioned authority. He also emphasized the importance of *praxis* and looked to the development of a discipline that is not marked by the insistence that there is only one approach to its subject matter.

Attention to phenomenology as a mode of ethical analysis has appeared in two papers dealing with foundational matters. In 1975 E. Clinton Gardner discussed "Phenomenological Analysis and Normative Ethics in Selected Theological Ethicists." The ethicists studied were Thielicke,

Løgstrup, H. R. Niebuhr, Mandelbaum, and Winter. Two years later Thomas Ogletree's paper, "The Claims of the Other: A Phenomenological Account of the Meaning of Moral Experience," (appearing in *The Selected Papers 1977* as "Hospitality to the Stranger") explored the relationship of selfhood and socialization with special reference to the work of Immanuel Levinas, who was concerned with the significance of the other as a moral actor for the development of the moral self. While appreciatively explicating the views of Levinas, Ogletree took issue with him for seeming to deny the reality of a moral agent before its encounter with the other, and cited Tillich's thinking on this matter as a helpful alternative. In 1969 William M. Longsworth gave a paper with the broad title, "Religious Beliefs and Moral Judgments." In this paper he acknowledged the independence of religion and morality while pointing to the fact that in practical ways religious beliefs and moral judgments overlap. He focused on recognizable interrelations at the level of discourse, identified five sets of variables that affect those interrelations, and illustrated how these variables appear in the thought of the eighteenth century British theologian and ethicist, Samuel Clarke.

A number of other papers have dealt with a variety of moral and philosophical issues. Dianne M. Yeager's paper at the 1982 meeting, "Tragedy, Suffering, and Ethics," looked at the problem of universalizing a definition of the right and suggested that while it is relatively easy to get agreement about positions that are wrong, it is impossible to arrive at universal agreement concerning what is "right" in an ethical situation. John Badertscher dealt with foundational issues in 1982 in a paper called "Freedom and Virtues."

One of the things that can be learned from scrutinizing the ways in which the members of the Society have handled foundational issues is that many of them move rather freely and without great scruples from the philosophical to theological realms of discourse. Robert W. Bertram's paper, "Responsibility: A Confessional-Ethical Splice," is a case in point. Joseph Allen's treatment of "H. Richard Niebuhr's Value Theory" in 1963 would be hard to pigeon-hole under just one of the rubrics, even though it observed that Niebuhr himself thought of his work as primarily theological in genre. Roger Hutchison's 1983 paper, "Mutuality: Procedural Norm and Foundational Symbol," was an autobiographical account of the experience of mutuality and an appreciative portrayal of Gibson Winter's accomplishments in the book *Liberating Creation*. Both Bertram's and Winter's approaches might well be considered theological by many philosophers and philosophical by many theologians. The members of the

Society have, it seems, been more free to use a greater variety of approaches in their work than might have been the case had they been under peer pressure to be self-consciously concerned about some pure methodology for the discipline. In moving, therefore, to the next genre of papers dealing with foundational issues, we are not suddenly leaping across a gulf of clear and immutable dimensions.

Theologically Formulated Issues

A casual observer of the years we are discussing might think, given the publicity accorded to the movement, that the discussion of situation ethics was one of the most prominent aspects of recent ethical thinking. That judgment is not substantiated by an examination of the programs of the Society. To be sure, John C. Bennett did give a presidential address in 1961 on "Ethical Principles and the Context" and George H. Easter did give a paper in 1965 on "New Frontiers in Protestant Contextual Ethics," but these are the only papers in the entire period in which the terms "contextual" or "situational" figure as the central focus of attention. Easter's paper was a discussion of the types of contextualist ethics and even indicated in one section how principles were being reintroduced in much contextualist thought. The record simply does not indicate that the scholarly deliberations of the Society were at any time dominated by plumping for a situationalist way of thinking.

However, many of the issues germane to a broader approach to a relational ethic did get canvassed. Two papers dealt specifically with divine command morality and these have been published. Glen C. Graber's "Philosophical Basis for a Defense of 'Divine Command' Ethics" appeared the year after its presentation in a revised form in *The Journal of the American Academy of Religion* XLIII (March 1975): 62-69, and an article based on a reply to it by John P. Reeder is found in *The Journal of Religious Ethics* III (Spring 1975): 157-163. Janice Marie Idziak's paper, "Divine Command Morality: An Historical Reappraisal," presented after her book of readings on the subject was published by Edward Mellin Press in 1979, showed that the history of divine command morality has been sadly neglected. Along with the ethics of love and natural law theory it has been a major strain in Christian ethical thinking and does not depend upon asserting that the power of God is the primary quality of the Godhead in relating to human beings.

In 1965 Max Stackhouse asked in a paper, "The Role of Technical Data in the Formation of Ethical Norms and Judgments," whether technical data is useful for the definition of norms themselves, and not merely for the strategy used to apply norms in action. Stackhouse contended that the prevalent ethos in which any ethicist works so affects thinking about norms that it is necessary to make an empirical analysis of that ethos in order to understand them. Consequently, norms cannot be adequately comprehended only in theological or ontological frameworks. While we must not reduce Christian ethics to sociology alone, we must take into account technical data to see the provisional norms already operative in a given ethos, the societal factors involved in understanding that ethos, how the factors thus understood affect judgments, and the kind of data that may be important for looking to the future. This attention to empirical data does not, according to Stackhouse, warrant a total relativizing, historicizing, or situationalizing of norms nor a reduction of the ethical task to emotive or primarily existential responses. In 1978 Stackhouse was again, in dialogue with David Little, looking at similar issues. In a paper entitled "The Category of 'The Fitting' in Religious Ethics" he argued that there are not two, but three, modes of ethical discourse: the deontological (dealing with right and wrong); the teleological (dealing with good and evil); and the ethological (dealing with the fitting and the unfitting). Situationalists and contextualists are to be commended for calling renewed attention to the importance of the third way, but to be resisted in their efforts to make it alone the foundational methodology. Little put a stronger reliance on the Kantian element than Stackhouse, and warned that too great an emphasis on the fitting would tend to collapse ethics into sociology. Thomas Ogletree extended this discussion the following year with a paper, "The Conflict of Interpretations: A Challenge to the Ethics of the Fitting," published as "The Activity of Interpreting Moral Judgment," in *The Journal of Religious Ethics* 8 (Spring 1980): 1-26.

Several papers given before the Society have been concerned with natural law. In 1962 Donald V. Wade discussed "The Revival of Natural Law in Contemporary Protestant Ethics." The following year Douglas Sturm gave a presentation on "Naturalism, Historicism, and Christian Ethics: Toward a Christian Doctrine of Natural Law." His paper was published in *The Journal of Religion* XLIV, (January 1964): 40-51. Two years later, an invited guest, Robert Johann, presented a paper on "Natural Law and the Person." Johann had been asked to share with members of the group current trends in Roman Catholic thinking, but he preferred to offer a wider treatment. His paper indicated that while there are limitations to the traditional "natural law" theory and while its orientation needs radical modification, this modification situates the theory within a wider context that preserves its deepest insights intact.

Whether or not Paul Elmen took all these things in and pondered them is not clear, but his presidential address in 1966 on "Law and Miracle" did start with a reference to John Bennett's earlier presidential address and to Paul Ramsey's raising of similar concerns in the book published the previous year in Scotland under the title *Deeds and Rules in Christian Ethics*. Noting that both *Time* and *Commonweal* had just carried popular articles about this, Elmen indicated that he would like to have avoided entering the discussion, but found it impossible to do so. Elmen, however, did not simply rehearse the arguments, but added a unique dimension to it by contrasting law with miracles rather than with situations or contexts. A miracle, like a situation, is concrete, occurs in the singular, and interrupts the regularity of law. The category of miracle can, therefore, do justice to the uniqueness of each person and to the emergence of the radically new element in history. Elmen noted that if the exceptional is made the standard it is no longer the exceptional. Therefore, argued Elmen, only by keeping law and miracle in tension, without reducing either to the other, can the value of both for ethical thought be preserved.

Three years later the problem of norms was still of concern to the Society and a panel consisting of Frederick Carney, Arthur Dyck, Richard McCormick and Gibson Winter canvassed the subject, "Norms and Social Change." In 1974 James Bresnahan, with David Tracy responding, discussed "Karl Rahner's Ethics: Natural Law and the Teleological-Deontological Controversy;" this was published, in a revised form, in *The Journal of Religion* 56, (January 1976): 36-60. In 1977 Stanley Harakas treated "Natural Law in Christian Ethics: An Eastern Orthodox Perspective" and in 1981 Dennis P. McCann took "A Second Look at Middle Axioms." The first of these presentations was published in *The Selected Papers* and the second, in *The Annual*.

Methodology in doing Christian ethics was a major concern in the mid-1970s. Roger Shinn's presidential address in 1975 looked at "The Style of Christian Polemics" and in 1977 J. Philip Wogaman examined "The Integrity of Christian Ethics." In the intervening year a concurrent session was devoted to a look at Paul Ramsey's work, which has often been pivotally concerned with the role of norms in Christian ethics. For Ramsey's rejoinders at that session see *The Journal of Religious Ethics* IV (Fall 1976): 185-237. Shinn considered why the ethicist engages in both irenics and polemics, acknowledged the presence of empirical elements in the way ethicists go about their work, took account of the motives that influence those who do the arguing, and suggested a posture for engaging in moral argument without destructive self-righteousness. Wogaman, raising the question as to whether there is any intellectual integrity possible in Christian ethics, indicated that what we believe about reality as-a-whole reflects aspects of the reality we have experienced and tends to shape our idea of what lies beyond immediate experience. Contending that the historical figure of Jesus Christ is bound to be central to Christians in their understanding of reality, even though it does not constitute the only metaphor they use, Wogaman held that it is in some way special, and posed the question whether Christians can rely upon their metaphors of reality with intellectual integrity. While Wogaman acknowledged that Christians can agree with people of many other persuasions about a great many specific judgments, they need to be able to answer for the faith they hold with reference to their most central object of value.

In 1976 Max Stackhouse gave a paper entitled "Modes of Justification in Ethical Arguments." Ideas drawn from that paper can be found in "The Location of the Holy: An Essay on Justification in Ethics," *The Journal of Religious Ethics* IV (Spring 1976): 63-104. The relationship of Christology to ethics was discussed two other times on the programs. In 1969 E. Clinton Gardner's paper on "A Critique of Christocentric Models of Ethical Analysis" was an early version of a theme Gardner wrestled with for many years and finally published in his book *Christocentrism in Christian Social Ethics: A Depth Study of Eight Modern Protestants* (University Press of America, 1983) with a note of gratitude in the preface for the collegiality he has experienced in the life of the Society. In 1980 Max A. Myers gave a paper on "The Meaning of Christology for Ethics."

The remaining papers to be mentioned under the rubric of theological treatments cover widely separated issues that are not part of an identifiable stream of discussion. That in no way make them less important. Indeed, it may be a mark of creative originality to have produced a paper that do not fit into the same category as a lot of others. The record surely requires that they be listed, in the order they were given.

1971 Rubem Alves, "Crisis of Imagination in Western Ethics"
1978 Marjorie Maguire, "Immortality and Ethics"*
1979 Joseph Allen, "The Inclusive Covenant and Special Covenants"*
1979 James Gaffney, "Temptation as an Ethical Category"
1979 Robert M. Adams, *"Eros in Agape"*
1980 Rolf Ahlers, "Theology as Interested Knowledge"

1980 Paul F. Camenisch, "Gifts and Gratitude in Ethics"
1981 Raymond K. Anderson, "Christian Approaches to an Ethics of the Imagination"
1981 Gilbert Meilander, "Friendship and the Problem of Preferential Love"
1982 Elizabeth Bettenhausen, "Three Interpretations of Sin in Ethics"
1983 James T. Johnson, "*Agape* as Creator of Community: A Reorientation"

(The substance of the paper by James Gaffney was printed in the *Annual Proceedings of the Catholic Theological Society of America* [1980] under the title "Experimenting on Morality." The paper by Paul Camenisch was published in *The Journal of Religious Ethics* IX [Spring 1981]: 1-34. The paper by Meilander bears a title very similar to that of the first chapter in his book *Friendship: A Study in Theological Ethics* [University of Notre Dame Press, 1981]).

Personal and Social Factors in Morality

Linking treatments of psychological and sociological factors in moral understanding together may not seem entirely adequate, despite the fact that both are normative sciences, but there are precedents for doing so. When John Satterwhite entitled his 1971 presidential address with the rubric used for this section, he was pointing to the fact that these factors have often been linked together in the Society's deliberations. Satterwhite took up a theme from the presidential address of the previous year, in which James Gustafson had explored "The Burden of the Ethical: Reflections on Disinterestedness and Involvement." (Published in *The Foundation* LXVI (Winter 1970): 8-15.) Gustafson had commented on the relationship between action and reflection which had been of concern over the years to many members of the Society. His contention that the personal and the social cannot be separated was echoed by Satterwhite, who traced the Black religious experience as an instructive example of having kept these two factors together. Satterwhite held up the Black agenda to the whole membership as one worthy of its allegiance. To that point we shall be returning in chapter six.

The papers discussed in this section have been concerned in different ways with either the personal/psychological elements in morality or with the societal/sociological ones. Ralph Potter and Steven M. Tipton canvassed the interplay between these factors in 1983 in a session on the subject "Moral Anthropology: The Social Location of Modes of Ethical Reasoning." In the course of the years two papers have focused more specifically on moral development. In 1973 T. J. Bachmeyer considered "Christian Ethics and Developmental Psychology: Implications of the Thought of Lawrence Kohlberg." This paper explicated Kohlberg's six stages, showing how someone at each of the six might make a decision about an act of mercy killing. Bachmeyer saw in Kohlberg's work a description of moral growth which raises a question as to whether a theoretical treatment of Christian ethics couched primarily in universalized principles can be communicated to people who have not yet achieved a stage of moral growth enabling them to comprehend general principles. Bachmeyer also suggested that Kohlberg's theories help us to think through problems involving a compromise of ethical principles and to devise moral pedagogies. The two formalistic criteria of the good--universality and impartiality--are implicit in Kohlberg's theory. Bachmeyer published his argument "Ethics and the Psychology of Moral Argument" in *Zygon* VIII (June 1973): 82-95. In 1980, another paper on Kohlberg was presented by Walter E. Conn which was published later in *The International Philosophical Quarterly* XXI (December 1981): 379-389, under the title "Morality, Religion, and Kohlberg's 'Stage Seven'." This paper reported on and discussed the implications of Kohlberg's efforts to identify a seventh, or religious, stage in development. It may come as some surprise to realize that the programs of the Society have, perhaps as has the discipline of Christian ethics in general, paid little attention to moral development theory.

Societal issues have been treated more often, but in a great variety of ways. Certainly the programs of the Society of Christian Ethics have not approached these matters with the same self-consciousness about sociological method as might be expected in The Society for the Scientific Study of Religion. Some of the presentations have been theoretical, some autobiographical, and some have even consisted of speculative readings of the future. The list of papers in this category will show that diversity.

1962 Kenneth L. Smith, "The Churches and the Sociology of the Sixties"
1962 James Luther Adams, "The Evolution of My Social Concern"
1963 Edward L. Long, Jr., "The Concept of Power in the Radical Right"
1964 J. Philip Wogaman, "Ethics and Planned Social Change"
1965 A panel with James Luther Adams, James Gustafson and Widick Schroeder, "New Frontiers in Ethics Research"

1966 Franklin H. Littell, "Right Wing Threats to America: Historical Perspectives"
1967 Edward L. Long, Jr., "Emerging Trends in Social Policy"
1967 Paul Abrecht and Charles West, "Central Issues for Christian Ethics from the World Council of Churches' Conference on Church and Society"
1971 A panel with Donald Evans, Daniel Maguire, David Ramage and Gayraud Wilmore, "Legitimacy of the Social Authority of the Churches"
1975 Paul Abrecht, "On Society: New Directions in Ecumenical Social Ethics"
1977 Norman Faramelli, "The Religious, Social and Ethical Implications of Contemporary Socio-Biology"
1977 Stuart D. McLean, "The Implications of Reference Group Theory for Doing Ethics"

(Of these, McLean's paper is available in *The Andover Newton Quarterly* XVIII [March 1978]: 211-221).

The plethora of papers mentioned in this chapter reveals not only how many kinds of issues are of foundational interest to Christian ethicists but also how diverse are the ways in which they approach them. The account of the programs of the Society may take on greater manageability as we look at the ways the papers have dealt with specific social issues and problems.

6

Seeking to Understand Oppression

Following foundational issues, the topic to which the next largest group of papers given at the annual meetings of the Society has been devoted has been arbitrary group-related injustice. While the term "oppression" would not have been used in the early years of the Society's history, attention to the conditions it describes was never entirely missing. Under this heading are included papers dealing with the Black agenda, the women's movement, and the plight of several other disadvantaged, disenfranchised, or dispossesed peoples with which liberation thinking has been concerned. Some distinct changes in the way issues are canvassed are evident in the story to be told in this chapter, but the continuity of the problem is clear.

From Race Relations to the Black Agenda

At the founding meeting in 1959, a panel of seven, about half of it consisting of members of the Society and half of it guests, discussed "The Moderate's Strategy in Race Relations." The anachronistic quality of that title is something of a clue to the considerable change that has occurred in the last quarter century in the way such matters are discussed. The fact that all the members of the panel--Robert R. Brown, E. Clinton Gardner, Brooks Hays, Daniel O. Hill, W. Astor Kirk, Guy H. Ranson, and Will D. Campbell--were male, and all but one was white, did not seem as shocking to the Society in those days as it would today. Our consciousness about instances of oppression has been modified in important ways during the life of the Society even though the tragic realities have probably not abated very much.

Nothing in the records reveals what was said at the 1959 panel, though Will D. Campbell may have left a clue to the kind of thinking prevalent at the time in an article he published shortly after participating, under the title "The Role of Religious Organizations in the Desegregation Controversy" (*Union Seminary Quarterly Review*, [January 1961]: 187-196).

It was to be four years before the Society addressed this issue again, and the files are equally barren about what was actually said when the discussion resumed. In 1963 Henry Clark presented a paper, "New Configurations in Minority Group Social Action." Clark had been thinking much about this subject and would soon write two articles about it, undoubtedly reflecting to some extent the thinking he presented at the Society's meetings. ("Reflections on the Negro Revolt," *Union Seminary Quarterly Review* 19 (January, 1964): 107-22; and, "Thinking About the Unthinkable in Race Relations," *Social Action* 30 (May 1964): 17-22). A year later Donovan E. Smucker gave a paper entitled "The Negro Revolt in Chicago: A Study of Confrontation in the Power Structure." In 1965 Joseph Washington and Benjamin Payton jointly led a session on "New Frontiers in Race Relations." Payton's thinking at the time may be reflected in articles entitled "Civil Rights and the Future of American Cities," Social Action (December 1966): 5-11; and "New Trends in Civil Rights," *Christianity and Crisis*, 25 (December 13, 1965): 268-71.

The files get better starting with the 1968 meeting and the analysis of the problem becomes more pointed in Joseph Washington's "Ethical Effectiveness in Achieving Civil Rights." Washington contended that the white majority had long possessed the power to see that the Black minority be accorded its full civil rights and that the white majority had failed to effect any systemic change. Only when the bus boycott of 1955 forced the issue was progress begun. Washington detailed the reasons (or rationalizations) why the white majority does not voluntarily move toward ethical effectiveness in civil rights. He cited the fact that intellectual whites disagree on both the nature of the problem and on the objectives to be achieved. He showed the insufficiency of several proposed solutions generally offered by white thinkers. He called for the mobilization of white consciousness in a massive effort to repudiate the myths and break the structures that support a segregated social system. He pointed out that if there is no breakthrough on this, although some legal victories for desegregation may be technically won, the conditions in which "great expectations continually meet great disappointments" will continue with disastrous consequences.

When Preston Williams received the program for the 1969 meeting he circulated a memo to members of the Society charging, in essence, that the very blockages which Washington had identified in the life of the country-as-a-whole were operative within the life of the ASCE itself. Williams charged that the Society had failed to take account of the Black revolution and had not paid enough attention to the significance of the Black Church in American life. Williams's memo produced consequences in the program planning for 1970 and for the attention subseqently paid to Black concerns in the ongoing programs of the Society. While the 1969 meeting had already been arranged and hence could not be very well changed, the Board of Directors, acting in response to Williams's criticisms, initiated moves to meet at a Black seminary in 1970, to give major program attention to ethical issues in the racial crisis, to incorporate members of the Black community in planning the program, and to initiate special efforts to increase the number of Black members of the Society. It is this response that may account for the fact that the number of papers discussed in this chapter--the great majority of which are concerned with the Black agenda--constitutes approximately a fifth of the total substance of the Society's program in the first twenty-five years of its history.

The 1969 program provided for the Sunday morning plenary session to be devoted to an address on "The Ethics of Power and the Black Revolution" by Nathan Wright, Jr., Executive Director of the Department of Urban Work, Episcopal Diocese of Newark. Drawing upon both Aristotle and Stokely Carmichael, Wright showed how central human fulfillment is to ethical well-being. He outlined how American institutions (which he characterized as relief-oriented rather than fulfillment-oriented) seek to pacify the dissident spirit rather than to change the mores of society so as to enable growth. Even the kindly disposed and socially minded get caught in this syndrome, which basically prevents human beings, particularly those who are powerless, from becoming what they could be. Wright indicted the educational system for failing to empower minorities and suggested that the educational system fails at this point because the society does not feel it needs the participation of the dispossessed.

Exploring Blackness as self-awareness, Wright showed how he came to appreciate its importance while studying the Church Fathers in order to write a book on worship, and declared, "One historic role of the oppressed has been to recivilize and re-humanize the society which has occasioned their oppression." Wright identified himself as a conservative Republican, reported that Richard Nixon responded favorably to these ideas, and stressed how this agenda could be carried out in regenerative ways, combining elements of both the saintly and the prophetic roles. This address gave a moderate foretaste of the themes that would be central to the program the following year.

No program of the Society has ever been more completely

devoted to a single theme than that at the 1970 meeting, which was held at the Interdenominational Theological Center in Atlanta. Except for the presidential address, which has been noted in connection with foundational issues, and one of two papers on the Problem of Violence that was weighted heavily to War/Peace isssues, all of the papers at the 1970 meeting were focused on what came to be called the Black agenda. A workshop on training agents for social change was concerned with teaching techniques and will be reported under that category, though it also was obviously pertinent to the Black issue. It is fair to suggest, therefore, that the call to concentrate a meeting entirely on the matters raised by Williams in his memo was complied with in spirit.

The papers and their authors in 1970 were, in order of their place on the program.

"Malcolm X and Christianity," by Lawrence Lucas
"Martin Luther King: A Christian Ethical Assessment," by James T. Laney
"A Theology of Black Power," by James Cone
"Styles of Black Ethics,"* by Preston Williams
"Economic Power and the Black Community"* by Benjamin Payton and J. Philip Wogaman
"Violence and Non-Violence"* by James Lawson

(Of these papers those marked with an asterisk are in the archives. The material in two of them has been incorporated into publications. James Cone's paper was the basis of the first chapter of his book, *A Black Theology of Liberation* [Lippincott, 1970]; Preston Williams' paper is reflected to a significant extent in "Ethics and Ethos in the Black Experience," *Christianity and Crisis* 33 [May 31, 1971]: 104-109. The papers by J. Philip Wogaman and James Lawson were among those distributed to the members).

The Sunday morning plenary session was addressed by C. Eric Lincoln, whose topic was not announced. However, copies of his "How, Now, America?" from *Christianity and Crisis* 28 (April 1, 1968): 56-9, were made available to members in mimeograph form. A presentation by Al Denman, entitled, "Compensatory Justice," was not a paper at all, but a slide presentation showing that the claims of Blacks and native Americans for reparations for past discriminatory acts has substantial support in American tort law. Another interesting part of the program was a meeting arranged by Professor Jonathan Jackson with members of the student body of Clark College who told it "Like It Is."

Two panels were also included in the 1970 meeting. One on "Black Caucuses" was brought together Negail R. Riley of the United Methodist Church, Gayraud Wilmore of the United Presbyterian Church, and Brother Joseph Davis of the Black Catholic Caucus. In the other panel, Max Stackhouse and Charles Powers each discussed "The Black Manifesto." Stackhouse had made his position known in "Reparations: A Call to Repentance," which appeared just before the meeting in *The Lutheran Quarterly* 21 (November 1969): 358-80.

It is hard to capture with these bibliograhical details the exciting and sometimes tense atmosphere of this meeting. Its impact was heightened by its location, the newness for many of the ideas that were asserted, the cumulative affect of having a single theme to the agenda, and the events in the life of the country that had preceeded it for several years. As we have seen in Chapter Three, this meeting prompted the formation of the Task Force on White Racism, which had as its purpose the deliberate exploration of these issues on a continuing basis. In the remaining thirteen years of the Society's first quarter century there have only been two years without a treatment of Black related issues, and in most years there have been two or more presentations on this subject.

The papers that have explored these matters in subsequent years have had a variety of orientations. Some have further explored the element of power in the relationships of minorities to the majority and the problems of whites in responding to a situation for which they bear a significant burden of guilt. Just one year after the Atlanta meeting, Herbert O. Edwards presented "Christian Ethics and Racism: Examination of the Thought of Reinhold Niebuhr, John C. Bennett, and Paul Ramsey." In 1972, Robert Terry, under the intriguing title, "Active New Whiteness: Lighting a Damp Log," suggested that the shapers and formers of racial practices in American life were, for the most part, self professed liberals on the racial question. "Racism," Terry pointed out, "...is not just one problem among many in America, but a presupposition of the cultural, institutional, and power realities in which much American policy is made and remade." Terry showed the bankruptcy of white liberalism in dealing with racism--in an analysis quite parallel to that made by Joseph Washington in the paper he presented at the 1968 meeting. This same meeting heard Charles S. Brown present a paper on "Strategies of Power in Racial Encounters."

In 1974, Theodore R. Weber delivered a paper entitled "Racism: Collective Guilt and Individual Responsibility," an adapted version of which was published under the title, "Guilt: Yours, Ours, and Theirs," in *Worldview* 18 (February 1975): 15-22. Weber utilized H. R. Niebuhr's distinctions between external and internal history to deal with the strange fact that while many persons are not deliberately and culpably involved in racism in the usual moral sense, they do feel a sense of guilt for its perpetration and perpetuation. Any effort to create a new history, suggested Weber, needs to analyze and deal with this experience of guilt and its consequences for people's behavior.

The 1976 presidential address by Preston Williams, which was not (as most such addresses) published in *The Selected Papers*, dealt with the problems of racism, as did a paper by J. Deotis Roberts on "Civil Rights: The Unfinished Agenda."

In 1981 Alan T. Davis examined "Anglo-Saxonism: The Ethics of a Race Myth." An article with a similar title has been published as "The Aryan Myth: Its Religious Significance," in *Studies in Religion/Sciences Religieuses* 10 (1981): 346-351. Davis showed how the racism of the nineteenth century was promulgated largely with purported scientific backing, and warned that it may return in such a guise if we are not on guard. In 1983 Preston Williams looked at "Impartiality and Racism."

Three papers, the first in 1974, the second in 1976, and the third in 1980, have described concrete action programs designed to deal with racism. In the first of these, Joseph Hough and Daniel Rhoades spoke about "Project Understanding: An Evaluation of a Program to Combat Racism, 1969." In the second, Jane Cary Peck told about "Successful Social Change in School Desegregation: A Model and Case Study." Her report is printed in *The Selected Papers* for 1976. In the third, Alan B. Anderson and George Pickering described "The Issue of the Color Line: A View from Chicago,"--a report on Martin Luther King, Jr.'s move to Chicago to build a northern base and confront housing segregation. They spoke about the roles of James Bevel and William H. Moyer in the movement there. The account of the agreement worked out between King and Mayor Richard Daley is given and the reasons explained as to why it failed to produce the desired goal of open housing. In the authors' judgment the consequent sense of frustration was a key element in nudging the civil rights movement toward the embrace of Black power.

The life and work of Martin Luther King, Jr. has been the subject of three other papers. In 1970, Ervin Smith spoke about "The Ethics and Promise of Martin Luther King, Jr." The same year, Charles Teel gave "King's Disobedient Clergy: A Theological-Ethical Profile," and in 1982 John H. Cartwright, speaking in honor of King and in a plea to make his birthday a national holiday, suggested that King has too long been treated (somewhat patronizingly) more as a Baptist preacher than as a constructive theologian. While

Cartwright suggested that truly serious work on King's thinking remains to be done, his systematic ethic would come to be interpreted as an ethic of *humanitas*. Cartwright maintained that King's approach was premised upon a belief in the solidarity of the human race that made the preservation of "the other" the first moral law. This view of *humanitas* implies Christian vocation and commitment, and contends that the means for achieving moral ends must be essentially benevolent. In brief, King held that created relatedness is the basis for community and that justice and love must be interrelated. Enoch Oglesby and Peter Paris responded to this presentation at the opening plenary session.

In addition to the papers about racism, Black identity, and related issues, the programs have also included some sessions devoted to the Black religious experience in both its American and its African settings. In 1973 James Cone examined "Ethical Motifs in Black Religion in America," and in 1980 Peter Paris gave a paper on "The Social Teachings of the Black Churches." The paper by Paris is included in *The Selected Papers*. Paris also published an article "The Social Teaching of the Black Churches: A Prolegomena," in *The AME Zion Quarterly Review* 92 (January 1981): 2-12.

J. Deotis Roberts delivered a paper in 1971 entitled "African Religion and African Social Consciousness," a version of which is published under an almost identical title in *The Journal of Religious Thought* 29 (1972): 43-56. In 1973 John Mbiti was a guest of the Society and spoke about "Ethical Motifs in Black Religion in Africa." Of similar interest is the article by Mbiti, E. Schweizer, et. al. on "Faith, Hope, and Love in the African Independent Church Movement: An Ecumenical Discussion," *Study Encounter* 10 (SE/63 '74): 1-19. In 1979 Norman E. Thomas spoke on the subject "Church Leaders in the Zimbabwean Liberation Struggle." Related material can be found in an article "The Ethics of Bishop Abel Muzorewa," in *Religion in Life* 49 (Summer 1980): 178-194. The same year Heidi Hadsell gave a paper "Prophetic Leadership: the Moral Rhetoric of Nyerere." In 1982 Richard Tholin did an analysis of "U.S. Churches and Liberation in Africa: Angola 1961-1981," and a year later Robert W. Bertram considered "'Confession' Against Apartheid: Where Faith is Ethos." Bertram's paper described the predicament of those Christians in South Africa for whom opposition to the racial system has become a matter of fundamental belief.

It is clear that the Society has built up some momentum in the consideration of Black related issues--a momentum for which there is a continuing need.

The Treatment of Women's Concerns

The Society was much slower to give attention to Women's concerns in its programs than it was to give attention to the Black agenda. Indeed it was not until 1972 that a paper appeared on the program which dealt directly with women's liberation. In that year Penelope Washburn gave "An Ethical Overview of Women's Liberation." Beverly Harrison followed in 1974 with "Some Ethical Issues in the Women's Movement"--a paper which is in the archives. Harrison focused attention on the importance of the feminist movement for the modern socio-ethical situation. She indicated how the thrust of any new movement is often directed at gaining a position within the arena of moral discourse. The primacy given this thrust may simply override any attempt on its part to legitimate arguments according to established ways of thinking and acting. To expect new movements to legitimate their arguments in that way is to make them submit to the very framework of discourse that precludes them and their concerns. Accordingly, for the women's movement, as for similar liberation movements, the point of reference must be futuristic (or, "u-topic" in the literal meaning of that term). Harrison also pointed to the contradictions involved in any view of compassion or personal sensitivity that is not rooted in full and complete solidarity and mutuality between all groups. From 1930 to 1960, argued Harrison, even though women in general may have gained some personal freedom, as a group they actually lost ground in the public arena. Some women did struggle mightily against social side-effects of the Industrial Revolution, working with energy, devotion, and imagination in areas of public education, health care, and social service, but were excluded even more than they had been in the nineteenth century from participation and influence in the public sphere. The resulting dichotomy between private and public value systems adversely affects both men and women and should be of concern to both. Harrison suggested that the feminist consciousness can be a resource for the social deliverance of this society--but not by itself the vehicle of that deliverance. The women's movement is a resource for challenging the subtle and better nuanced forms of oppression that threaten human fullness in covertly orchestrated and gently mechanized ways rather than (as in nihilistic tyranny) in blatant and violent ways. Concluding, Harrison observed that much depends on whether a new reading of freedom enables those who have been oppressed (even in subtle ways) to demystify their condition, and whether the radical nature of freedom can recapture the lost connectedness of interpersonal relationships that are destroyed so readily in an objectivized world of technologism and manipulative politicism.

It was four years before the programs again devoted attention to women's concerns. At that time Jane Cary Peck convened a panel on "Rights, Justice, and Power in Feminist Perspectives." Another gap then occurred, also four years long, before the 1982 presidential address of Daniel C. Maguire and a paper by James S. Allen both addressed these issues at the same meeting. Maguire's address, which was printed in *The Annual* (but first appeared in *Christianity and Crisis* 42 (March 15, 1982): 59-67) described three kinds of sexism: 1) the blatant bias that openly asserts male superiority; 2) an insidious assumption that the feminine is an important corrective of masculine arrogance--but hardly a viable mode for the conduct of affairs in a "real" world; and, 3) a benign acceptance of feminism as a valid agenda for women. Noting that male dominance has brought the warring instinct into prominence in our culture, Maguire suggested five tendencies that preserve the "macho-male blight": 1) a proneness to violent modes of power; 2) a hierarchial proclivity that is antithetical to community; 3) a tendency to abstraction that makes it possible to hate enemies and to neglect present human needs while pursuing futuristic goals; and, 4) a consequentialism which easily becomes "bottom line" thinking; and 5) a hatred which expresses itself in the systemic exclusion of women from many desirable roles.

Observing the extent to which Christian ethics has for the most part been male-dominated and the tendencies to abstract intellectualizing that have consequently become central to the discipline, Maguire suggested that something very profound--which he called feminization--is ocurring in our culture. This is infiltrating the affective, subliminal, and genetic regions of understanding with elements of healing appreciation. This will serve theology well, since in the past the mystical element has been a part of theology at its profoundest. Faith is a child of affection--as Thomas Aquinas knew so well. The use of male language for God, for which Maguire found no warrant other than a false ontology and a false cosmology based on masculinity, becomes the final symbol of the problem. It makes power more crucial than love in thinking about the attributes of ultimacy. "When a healed masculine and feminine blend into a more genuine humanity," concluded Maguire, "we [and our discipline] will be better."

In his paper, James Allen indicated the basic hostility among many church groups, especially the Orthodox, Roman Catholic, and the Mormon Churches, and among the new religious right, to the challenges which the women's movement is making. He urged mainline Protestants to think clearly to a position of support for the objectives of the women's movement in relation to the functions of the family, the role of the reproductive process, and the nature of work.

In 1983, Lisa Sowle Cahill looked at the terms "'Male' and 'Female' in Normative Ethics." In a long paper, she examined both the Genesis creation stories and the results of empirical investigation to see that "sexual differention as male and female is good, is part of humanity as created (human 'nature'), and is not incompatible with the inclusion of both male and female in what is meant by 'image of God.'" The paper by Professor Schüssler Fiorenza, which was discussed in the last chapter, was also a contribution to the same agenda.

Despite the high quality of these individual contributions, it does not seem that the women's issue has as yet been canvassed in the programs of the Society as fully as it needs to be. The extent to which thinking about these issues can lead to a broad new way of thinking about ethics was well demonstrated by the 1983 presidential address of Beverly Harrison. Harrison identified the fundamental theological hermeneutic underlying various liberation theologies and showed how they gained methodological distinctiveness by recognizing that our knowledge of God is grounded in the concrete struggle of persons to realize right relationships with each other in communitarian social conditions. While she acknowledged other widely held criticisms of liberation theology and its approach to ethics, she focused on the defense of its substantive theological claim that a *praxis* of right-making relationships is a pre-condition for ethical discernment in theology. She identified the conception of persons and politics implicit in the liberation paradigm, contrasting it with elements in the reigning liberal outlook. In conclusion she invoked a feminist analysis of physical embodiment as the specific linkage between our longing for justice and the conditions for realizing mutuality, or love.

These several efforts to bring women's concerns to the attention of the Society warrant the expectation and hope that the future will find a great deal more attention being given to these concerns.

The Self-Identity and Liberation of Other Groups

This subsection may be something of a potpourri, for the themes of oppression, liberation, and group identity as a foundation for ethical reflection move into many by-ways. One way they seem not to have moved in the programs of the Society, however, is into attention to gay rights. Except for one paper, more germane to sexual morality than to gay liberation, that issue has not been the focus of concern for any paper given at the Society.

Ethnic identity was given attention in a 1972 panel consisting of Geno Baroni, Joseph N. Davis, Gabriel Fackre, and Michael Novak on the subject "Ethnic Values and Social Change." Gabriel Fackre's ideas on this occasion were later incorporated into an article, "Archie Bunker: Visions and Realities," published in *The Christian Century* 89 (July 19, 1972): 772-4. In that article Fackre showed that Archie is human too, and is striving for a chance to shape his own future as much as those members of minorities that are vocal about oppression. Archie's striving often takes the form of a rising anger against technological dehumanization and may in time make common cause with others striving to be free--those very others with whom Archie now seems to want nothing to do. Michael Novak's ideas were later incorporated into an article, "How American Are You if Your Grandparents Came from Slovakia in 1888?," which was published in *Soundings* LXVI (Spring 1983): 1-20. Novak, citing Geno Baroni's work, showed that both Black and white minorities have been defrauded by society and hence each has more to gain from cooperation with the other than from hostility and antagonism.

In 1977 Terence Anderson delivered a paper, "Issues of Justice in Native American Land Claims," which seems to be the only attention paid in the programs to the problems of this group.

Concern about human rights is integrally related to the focus of this chapter, but it is so often treated in the context of international affairs that we will place the main discussion of it in the next chapter. But we will note that Sister Isabel Letelier's address to the Sunday morning plenary session at the 1981 meeting on the subject "Ethics and Politics of Liberation: An Agenda for the Eighties" focused in that direction. Her paper, which was delivered just two days before the inauguration of Ronald Reagan, foretold with great accuracy the changes that were to come in U.S. policy toward Latin and Central America. It indicated how United States support for military regimes of an intensely repressive quality (simply because they oppose "the cancer of Communism") creates liberation movements throughout the region that are opposed to all violence, systemic as well as overt, that of the United States as well as that of Russia. She pled with members of the Society to understand the struggle of these groups.

It is surprising how few papers have considered liberation theology in the South American context. In 1979, Carol Robb looked at the "Ethical Procedures of Gutierrez and Alves," and her paper was published in *The Selected Papers*. She entered the debate between those who see Christian social ethics as a truly interdisciplinary undertaking and those who see it as involving a more explicitly philosophical exploration of moral discourse. Turning to the work of two South American liberation theologians, she noted that, while both acknowledge the importance of their historical standing ground for doing ethics, they differ in methodology and conclusions. According to Robb, Alves contends that human fulfillment as the goal of orthopraxis must at this point remain undefined, while Gutierrez believes that "the criteria for liberation can only be defined in the context of a world-wide class analysis." Gutierrez is willing to postulate a greater place for middle axioms than Alves. A paper like that of Robb indicates how much we need more solid analysis of liberation theology with the tools that are possessed by the Society's membership.

The discussion of liberation has, as we have seen, brought up issues that are germane to international affairs, foreign policy, and questions of war and peace. Papers dealing with those categories constitute the next largest genre of material from the programs and will be discussed in the next chapter.

7

War/Peace Issues and International Relations

The period between the two world wars was marked by a rising surge of optimistic pacifism. This in turn brought forth several highly articulate efforts by major theologians to counteract that optimism by taking note of Augustine's understanding of the behavior of the City of this World. Even the most realistic reading of events that could have been imagined in the period from 1919 to 1943 would never have contemplated the sustained tension, the embrace of military answers as the prime resort, and the reliance upon the ultimate destructiveness of a nuclear arsenal, all of which have increasingly come to furnish the context for thinking about issues of war and peace during the period from 1959-1983.

Thinking About the Morality of War in the Sixties

The year 1961 was the first year in which the program of the Society dealt with the moral problems raised by war. Paul Ramsey gave a paper entitled "The Just War and the Nuclear Dilemma." This paper came out of the work he was doing to prepare his chapter in *Nuclear Weapons and the Conflict of Conscience, John C. Bennett, ed., (Scribners, 1962), and contained a working version of the "Hatfield and McCoys" parable that subsequently appeared in chapter eight of his own book, The Just War* (Scribners, 1968). A year later, a panel consisting of Ernest W. Lefever, William A. Banner, and Culbert Rutenber looked at "Christian Ethics and Foreign Policy." Lefever entitled his contribution "Basic Issues in Foreign Policy." Both Banner and Rutenber entitled their contributions "Critiques of the Christian Realist Approach to Foreign Policy."

The presidential address for the next year was given by Paul Ramsey on "Deterrence During War: a Portion of a Paper on 'Thinking About the Do-able and the Un-do-able.'" Ramsey contended that the right of reprisal cannot be an all-embracing rule that legitimates the suspension of other criteria for determining what is just or unjust in war, though he pointed out that in the past the very willingness to create an expectation that reprisals in kind will occur has often prevented grossly unjust actions by nation states from arising in the first place. Referring to the problems posed by massive stockpiling of nuclear weapons, Ramsey observed, ". . . the situation today is that the irrationality and purposelessness of pure punishment is laid bare before all eyes to see, together with the fact that the spiritualization of war into a contest of resolves is literally the most abysmal of all wars we could contemplate. One can still contemplate it, but it cannot be done except as an act that no longer has political purpose."

Ramsey's purpose in this address was to examine the immense moral problems created by weapons of mass destruction. While Ramsey clearly contended that nuclear weapons are not to be employed against civilian populations or other noncombatant targets, he resisted the logic that the nuclear pacifists were using to move from the moral unacceptability of counter-population retalitation to the repudiation of all forms of nuclear warfare. Ramsey seemed quite confident a fundamental distinction could be maintained in practice between threats to retaliate against whole populations and threats to retaliate only against nuclear forces.

Much of the 1964 meeting was given over to the discussion of the ways in which the development of nuclear weapons was affecting traditional thinking about the morality of war. The Friday afternoon plenary session was devoted to the general theme, "The 'Post-Christendom' Situation and Christian Ethics." Paul Peachey saw in the new situation an opportunity for Christians to legitimize a stance toward the culture not dissimiliar to the stance of early Christians toward the political order in their time--a stance involving the repudiation of war as an act of conscience. Peachey later published "New Ethical Responsibility: The Task of Post-Christendom Ethics," *Interpretation* 19 (January 1965): 26-38. At this same meeting a Saturday morning plenary session involved four members of the Society in "A Re-examination of 'Realistic Ethics.'" Since Christian realism had become so central in providing the intellectual scaffolding with which these issues were framed in those days, this panel focused on foundational aspects of the problem. Daniel Rhoades, who spoke on "The Prophetic Insight and the Theoretical-Analytical Inadequacy of Christian Realism," directed much of his attention to Reinhold Niebuhr's thought, and Samuel Magill spoke about "Some Significant Contributions in the Political Realism of Hans Morgenthau." Rhoades suggested that Niebuhr's attempt to make the doctrine of human nature the clue to political thinking rendered his scheme blind to certain kinds of social pathology. Magill, explicating Morgenthau's view of politics as the process of arriving at viable balances between conflicting claims, pointed to the contrasting ingredients in Morgenthau's thinking, ingredients that revealed a sensitivity to the need to control and direct power as well as the need to recognize its importance. "Morgenthau," noted Magill, "knows that shared power and interest must always undergird a viable political organization." According to Magill, Morgenthau has not been merely a power philosopher, but a realist who has carefully weighed the rich possibilities as well as the inadequacies of the human capacity to create community. John Swomley responded to Rhoades with a remarkable sense of agreement and Wilmer Cooper responded to Magill by suggesting that Morgenthau's thinking posed far greater problems for a Christian ethic than Magill seemed to realize.

The programs in both 1966 and 1967 devoted a considerable proportion of time to the discussion of war/peace issues. An unprecedented program format was tried--one that depended upon everyone reading materials in advance. (It might be noted that this format was abandoned after those two years). In 1966, William V. O"Brien, Director of the Institute of World Polity, Georgetown University, was invited to share a position paper that he had previously given as part of a seminar for the Council on Religion and International Affairs. His paper was distributed in advance to all members of the Society, as were written responses from Quentin Quade, Paul Deats, Vernon Ferwerda, Robert Gessert, Paul Peachey, and Paul Ramsey. Nearly a hundred pages of single-spaced copy was thus made available to members before the meeting, but nothing in the record indicates how fully this material was read.

O'Brien's paper, dealing with the morality of counter insurgency warfare, showed how utterly disruptive insurgency warfare can be. He characterized it as being primarily concerned with bringing down an existing order rather than working toward a constructive political alternative, and noted that persons of good will seeking constructive solutions are frequently assassinated or destroyed by such conflict. The moral problem raised by the appearance of this kind of warfare are enormous, since its unprecedented terrorism seems to call for reactive measures that are incompatible with the traditional standards of civilized behavior. O'Brien explored whether it was right to engage in the massive bombing of civilian and non-combatant targets if that seemed the only way to counter insurgency warfare, whether it would be just to employ torture to extract information about the tactics of insurgents if doing so were the only way to prevent them from inflicting massive damage upon a society, and whether there is any possibility of achieving anything even remotely resembling traditional victory from entering into such unconventional conflicts.

While it is not clear how widely O'Brien's paper or the responses to it were read before the meeting, it is clear that Theodore Weber did read these materials with care as background for leading the session. He prepared a paper entitled "Wars of National Liberation: the Methodology of Christian Ethics." Weber's paper indicated how the various responses looked at the issues raised by O'Brien's presentation. It became the basis for the first hour of discussion at the annual meeting, and was subsequently published in two concurrent issues of *Worldview* 9 (June 1966): 7-12; and (July/August 1966): 15-19, where it can be consulted for a fuller report on Weber's findings.

Weber showed how the responses to O'Brien's paper lined up according to the long-standing (and unresolved) differences between Christians about their proper role in politics. His scale put eschatological fidelity to Jesus Christ at one end--occupied by Paul Peachey--and obligations to the political claim of the nation-state--represented by Robert Gessert--at the other end. Weber also examined each response to O'Brien's paper to discern its attitude to the morality of intervention in wars of national liberation. Here a similar spectrum turned up, with pacifists like Peachey and Deats very wary about such intervention, and others, like Quentin Quade and Robert Gessert, justifying it as part of the effort to contain Communist expansionism. Weber noted the absence from the panel of a significant nonpacifist opponent of intervention, which at that time would have included persons like Hans Morgenthau, Walter Lippmann, or John C. Bennett. Reading these papers and Weber's analysis many years later makes one realize how persistent are these issues.

A year later, the Society was again discussing the moral dilemmas of intervention, likewise in an unprecedented and never-repeated format. Five concurrent sessions were arranged under the general rubric, "Revolution and the Third World: Problems in Ethics." William J. Cook, who helped arrange this part of the program, began the Saturday afternoon period with a fifteen-minute introduction to the five different topics into which the subject had been divided. The five topics were: Revolution and Development; Revolution and Security in Developing Areas; Revolution and Ideology; Revolution and International Order; Revolution and U.S. Policy. Each of the concurrent sessions discussed from one to three previously prepared and previously distributed papers. All told, twenty-seven people were involved in leadership roles for this part of the program. Clearly the matter was of great concern to warrant so heavy an involvement on a topic for a second year in a row.

In the late nineteen sixties no group concerned with social issues could escape the impact of the Vietnam War. Deep differences of opinion concerning the legitimacy of American involvement in that conflict were racking the country and were likewise present in the membership of the Society. While there were no papers given before the Society that argued a particular position on the war in the same frontal way that action groups were calling attention to the issue in the society outside, many members of the Society would allude in one way or another to their own position on the matter. Ralph Potter's paper at the 1968 meeting did address the problems of the time, but more by taking a long serious look at the debate rather than jumping into one side of it. Under the title, "New Problems for Conscience in War," Potter explored the tests of adequacy that should be applied to discourse about the morality of war, and how moral considerations interrelate with policy decision-making in a complex and pluralistic society. Warning against political punditry and ethical journalism, Potter canvassed the theoretical frameworks provided by classic Christian explorations of these matters and indicated the conditions that would contribute to cogency and fairness in moral discourse about war. The kind of reflection Potter shared with the Society is further developed in the book which he published shortly thereafter, *War and Moral Discourse* (John Knox Press, 1969), and in an article, "The Moral Logic of War," *The McCormick Quarterly* 23 (May 1970): 203-33.

Two papers that were presented during the sixties cannot be properly described as discussions of the morality of war, but rather would be reported as discussions of the making of public policy about international relations. In 1963, William J. Cook, in a paper entitled "U.S. Publics and Foreign Policy Processes," examined how foreign policy gets made and the processes that Christian ethicists and church groups should take into account in seeking to have an influence over such policy. Cook proposed a theory of an "intervening elite" that includes policy makers, trained experts, and even the leaders of the Churches. This intervening elite has a significant role to play in exerting an influence upon the values and moods of the mass public as well as upon the thinking of those who do the governing. He stressed the importance of developing a sophisticated understanding of the processes by which foreign policy is formed, an understanding that would match the sophisticated grasp of moral issues already found among Christian ethicists.

In a quite different way, Theodore Weber was raising issues about the adequacy of the Christian political understanding of the international situation in the late 1960s. His paper at the 1968 meeting, entitled "Reconciliation and Foreign Policy," while disassociating itself from "theologies of messianism" which prod Christians to embrace revolutionary activities in the name of liberation, searched for a way of thinking about political life that offered a better hope than those realisms that see politics only as a means of administering force. Noting that the significance of reconciliation was neglected both by those privatized interpretations of the Gospel that make it a matter of individual salvation and by those theologies that deny the possibility of reconcilation in macro-relationships, Weber called for the civilizing of power as a means of making a more peaceful world. His reasoning, hardly well developed in either the sixties or the seventies, may yet be heard again if attention moves from thinking about war as a problem for the Christian conscience to thinking about the making of peace as a form of Christian stewardship.

Different Strands in the Discussions from 1970 to 1983

Thinking about issues related to war and peace in the period from 1970 to 1983 proceeded on several different tracks.

1) The discussion of pacifism. This topic continued to attract occasional attention. In 1977, Walter Bense gave a paper on "The Pacifism of Karl Barth: Some Questions for John H. Yoder." (Yoder was there to answer the questions.) Bense's paper is published in *The Selected Papers*. The same year, Glen Stassen gave a paper which examined the experiences of those who protested against the Vietnam War and showed the ways in which participating in those protests had been an educational experience for them. Given at the meeting as "Justice and the Debates Over Amnesty," this paper was published with the title "Amnesty and Fairness" in *Power and Empowerment in Higher Education*, D. B. Robertson, ed. (University of Kentucky Press, 1978): 107-133. In 1980 Duane Friesen looked at "Refusing to Pay Taxes as Protest Against Military Expenditures." In its own way, each of these papers enhanced the understanding of the problem of the private individual who finds participating in war morally impossible, but they are not indicative of the main directions that the presentations of war/peace issues at the programs of the Society took after 1970.

2) Arms Policy. Another strand in the discussion of war/peace issues and international affairs since 1970 focused on arms policy and disarmament questions, with a

particular emphasis on the problems of nuclear weapons. In 1975 Bryan Hehir gave a paper with the title "The New Nuclear Debate: Political and Ethical Considerations," which was published in *The Selected Papers*. Hehir examined the debate about nuclear weapons as it was carried out from 1958-1968 and then detailed the new technological, political, and strategic factors that in his judgment had reshaped the moral issue to the point where the structural framework used for past discussions had become outdated. Hehir's paper was a skillful encapsulation, not only of the difference in the old debate between positions such as Paul Ramsey's (favoring a limited concept of deterrence) and the nuclear pacifism of the writers in W. Stein's *Nuclear Weapons and the Conflict of Conscience*, but also of the differences discernable between Frederick Ikle and Herbert Scoville over the implications of Ballistic Missiles and Multiple Independently Targetable Re-Entry Vehicles (MIRVs). Considering the intense moral issues raised by the concept of Mutual Assured Destruction (MAD), Hehir advanced a position toward it that justified mounting a nuclear threat by developing such weapons while withholding moral sanction for their use. He acknowledged the problem of credibility in a position legitimizing the acquisition but not the use of weapons and admitted that he saw no way around the difficulty. He also decried the loss of interest in the debate and pleaded for the integration of the nuclear issue with a consideration of global justice and peace. Hehir's subsequent contribution to the discussion of these issues through his own writing and staff work for the Roman Catholic bishops has become widely known.

Five years later, in 1980, James Johnson gave a paper, "Weapons Limits and the Restraint of War: A Just War Critique." Like Hehir's paper, this was also printed in *The Selected Papers*. Johnson argued that the just war tradition furnishes the most fitting base on which to restrict the development and possession of weapons. He provided a running account of certain historical efforts to limit or restrain particular weapons--most of which were produced by an advancing technology--and he noted the similarities and the differencs between efforts to ban gas and outlaw bacteriological weapons and the efforts to arrive at limitations on nuclear weapons. Like Hehir, he found a carefully stated warrant for developing a nuclear capability strictly for its deterrent effect against attack *per se*, but could come up with no moral legitimation for the use of such a capability should it fail as a deterrent. The issues explored by both Hehir and Johnson in these papers were later to become the subject of greater public attention.

In 1982 Theodore J. Koontz gave "An Ethical Analysis of

the Salt II Debate." At the time of its presentation this was a preliminary report on dissertation research. It looked at the general problem of Salt II, the views of the major powers, the sources of their disagreements about issues, and even more particularly, at the debate within the United States about the legitimacy and significance of the talks. It examined the thinking of three senators: Henry Jackson, Joseph Biden, and Mark Hatfield. Like the paper of William Cook in 1963, this study directed attention to the way foreign policy matters are dealt with in the American political process. The next year, Paul Bock, who had just returned from a stay in Europe, reported on "The Nuclear Debate within German Protestantism." His report was mainly about the discussion taking place in the West German church--a debate that was deeply dividing its membership. It was helpful to hear how the discussions of these matters are carried out by Christians in other nations.

3) The Problem of Violence in General. During the seventies attention came to be focused less upon international conflict by itself and more upon violence as a general problem for the Christian conscience. In 1970 both James Lawson and Franklin Sherman presented papers entitled "Violence and Nonviolence." Both of these papers were distributed in mimeographed form to the membership after the meeting. Lawson showed that both our history as a nation and the climate of opinion that was prevalent at the time so shaped our thinking that we seldom even began to think of alternatives to violence in seeking social change. Terming racism, poverty, and violence "the social trinity of evil," Lawson argued that these three systems of cruelty are welded to each other in an interlocking web that engulfs the whole world in its grip. He suggested that a less exploitative society might be able to overcome violence, but that the American war machine was blocking the development of such a society both at home and abroad. He criticized those who glibly support violent revolutionary movements and argued for the moral superiority of nonviolent direct action as a means of securing social change. His presentation contains a list of similarities and contrasts between violence and nonviolence as instruments of conflict.

Sherman examined the issue in the light of two documents: 1) a lecture by John P. Spiegel, a Brandeis Professor of Social Psychiatry, and 2) the volume by H. D. Graham and T. R. Gurr prepared as a report to the National Commission on the Causes and Prevention of Violence (the Eisenhower Commission). Sherman admitted that violence may be "normal" in the statistical sense, but held that it can never be "normal" in the moral sense. He made a sharp distinction between an "expressive" type of violence that cannot have a moral purpose, and a "programmed" violence that can be brought under scrutiny and restraint. Any resort to violence that is to fit the second category (as a last resort in a just war, for example) must be undertaken with a sense of failure that prompts regret and contrition even while pleading its necessity. Arguing that just war teaching brings together a reading on empirical conditions with moral judgments as to when violence may possibly be justified, Sherman suggested that a similar process must be developed for judging when resort to violence might be warranted in other cases. While eschewing a pacifism that rules out all violence on *a priori* grounds, Sherman indicated that there are serious reasons for questioning the endorsements of violence as a means of social change that were prevalent in some church circles at the time he wrote. His paper refers the reader to a discussion of other aspects of the problem published as "Theological Reflections on Violence," *Dialog 8* (Winter, 1969): 25-32.

A year later, a panel on the subject "Violence as a Proper Means of Social Change: Historical Perspectives," provided another set of insights for thinking about this subject. C. Freeman Sleeper gave a presentation on "Perspectives on Violence in Early Christianity;" John E. Lynch, a paper on "Violence and Social Change in the Middle Ages;" and David Little, a paper on "Some Justifications for Violence in the Puritan Revolution." These papers were also distributed in mimeographed form to the membership of the Society after the meeting. Each of them illustrates how valuable it can be to examine a contemporary issue by noting historical precedents, providing one guards against simplistic parallelisms. It was Sleeper's main contention that the New Testament writers were facing the question of order in terms relating to the new Christian movement rather than the political order of the time, and that therefore their comments about violence cannot be used as guidance for contemporary political questions without a most imaginative (and therefore most hazardous) transpositioning of the framework. Lynch traced how the growth of the cities as locations for a new commercial class developed a new kind of voluntary association which gave rise to struggles (and attendant violence) against the old order. The peasants also became involved in these struggles against feudalism. Lynch asked, "How do we distinguish between a violence that liberates and a violence that enslaves?" He indicated the great difficulty of answering that question when one is very close to a conflict. David Little's paper took issue with the interpretation of the Puritan Revolution given by both

Roland Bainton and Michael Walzer, who saw it as the abandonment of just war doctrine and the embrace of a crusade ethic. Instead, Little showed that the shift is better described as a change in just war teaching to make the consent of the governed a central test of political justice--though he did acknowledge that some holy war rhetoric crept into the discourse of the time.

In 1976 Walter Muelder presented a discussion of the problem of violence with reference to discussions about this issue taking place in the World Council of Churches. Six years before *The Readers Digest* oversimplifed the matter, Muelder gave a careful analysis of the problems facing the World Council of Churches as it came to grips with the vast complexity of violence in modern society and the manifold ways in which the problem arises in different parts of the world. This paper, which was published in *The Selected Papers*, posed several questions that ought to be faced both by those espousing violence as a necessary means of social change and by those advocating nonviolence as a path of moral purity.

4) The World Situation. At the same 1976 meeting several other papers dealt with war/peace concerns from a variety of perspectives. Ernest Lefever dealt with "Intelligence, Secrecy, and a Free Society." Rena Karefa-Smart asked "Is Democracy Viable in the Third World?" These papers are not available to be reported upon. Donald W. Shriver, Jr. considered "Survival Ethics: The Question of Triage." His paper, which is available in *The Selected Papers* under the title "Lifeboat Ethics: The Case for Mainlanders," examined the logic of triage (which was worked out in wartime for dealing with the wounded in military hospitals) and showed that it does not provide an adequate basis for judging our moral reposibilities toward a hungry and impoverished world. Shriver saw triage as misleading because it is an ethic of what to settle for rather than an ethic of what to strive for, which therefore encourages a too ready acquiescence to harsh and inhumane realities that may not indeed be the final circumstance of persons on this planet. This paper was also published in *Soundings* 59 (Summer 1976): 234-243.

Twice in the middle seventies the Society devoted attention to problems of world poverty and development in plenary sessions with guest speakers. In 1974 Denis Goulet, the author of *The Cruel Choice* and *A New Moral Order*, was asked to address the membership on "Christian Ethics and World Development: A Critical Perspective." Jan Milic Lochman responded. Goulet's paper was distributed to the Society in mimeographed form with a request that it not be cited. Those who were there will remember it as a careful delineation of the value crisis produced by the thrust toward development and a plea that Christian ethicists not yield to any simplistic reductionism that makes politics, revolution, or economic well-being into the only touchstones for policy. In responding to Goulet's paper, Lochman indicated his own *Sitz in Leben* as a person living in the "Second World" and suggested that the inertia of people in that world is as great as in the "First World." Calling for Christian ethicists to break through the "consumer mentality" that dominates in both situations, Lochman asked that they develop a theological perspective that places the solidarity of all the human race at the center of concern, that they provide a critical prophetic vision opposing all naive or arrogant identification of the human with the patterns of any one culture, and that the values of an innerworldly restraint be rediscovered as a foundation for living in mutuality with others in the world. Lochman argued that the world must rediscover that the way of self restraint is the way of survival.

Two years after Goulet spoke to the Society, Professor Ronald Mueller of American University spoke to another Sunday morning plenary session on "Global Interdependence, Social Stability, and the Future of U.S. Democracy: The Dovetailing of Ethics and the Human Sciences." As is true of too many of the guest presentations, this has not been made part of the record, and the benefits of having such a guest expert have been limited to those who attended the session. In 1977 a panel with James Will and James Finn was held on the subject, "The Future of East-West Relations: Is 'Detente' Dead?" There may have been more detente at that panel than there would be if these two individuals were to engage in the same discussion today, since the disagreements about the wisest way to deal with the polarized world situation have become considerably sharper in the intervening years.

Along the way two sessions have been devoted to the teaching of peace concerns. These will be reported on in the chapter dealing with teaching. Moreover, there has been a good deal of attention paid to human rights as an international concern. The papers dealing with that subject will be treated in the chapter on the Society's thinking about politics and law.

8

Politics, Law, and Human Rights

Christian ethicists have generally made the study of political affairs an important focus of attention. Indeed, political considerations thread their way through many of the papers that have already been discussed in previous chapters, as for example, in those papers that examine how power is used as an instrument of oppression and in those papers that explore the relationships between Christian theology and Marxist thought. But a significant group of papers given before the Society has focused more directly on the nature and function of politics as a subject of exploration in its own right. These will be discussed in the first section of this chapter.

Another group of papers to be considered in this chapter has been concerned with the nature of law. There is a curious relationship between politics and law. Both are concerned with the ordering of society. Both are concerned with the achievement of justice. Both pay attention to how interactions between individuals and groups can be made to serve certain ends. Both can be instruments of corruption and be used in less than honorable ways, so that the terms "politicized" and "legalistic" have equally unsavory implications. Yet, the study of politics differs from the study of law. Politics is concerned with gaining and holding control over government for the attainment of specific ends. Law is concerned with establishing and maintaining legitimacy for the system of government in its entirety. The final appeal in politics is the election booth; in law, the the courtroom. Politics depends on persuasion and coercion while law depends upon precedent and legitimation. Politics is more operational than law; law is more procedural than politics. In politics power is used as a means of control; in law one of the more important concerns is to control power. In politics, partisanship is crucial and advocacy is the servant of causes; in law, advocacy is a means of obtaining justice and is considered a special trust that stands above partisanship. Thus, while political philosophy and legal philosophy bear a close resemblance, they cannot be collapsed into each other without doing violence to the central characteristics of each. The adequately informed ethicist must be at home with the discourse and insights of both.

A third part of this chapter will deal with human rights. The protection of human rights may be the highest calling of both politics and law, and the discussion of human rights, a unique place for ethics, politics, and law to interact with one another.

The Treatment of Politics in the Programs of the Society

The 1961 meeting of the Society was opened with a panel on "Religion and the Political Order, 1960." G. McLeod Bryan, George W. Forell, E. Clinton Gardner, T. B. Maston, and John W. Turnbull were scheduled to participate, but only Gardner and Maston were able to attend. Even so, all five submitted materials that were included in the 1960-61 *Yearbook*.

The situation which these four persons addressed was an unprecedented one. John F. Kennedy had been elected the first Roman Catholic president of the United States less than three months before this meeting. The Society was by no means the only group discussing the implications of this event, but the amount of space given to the discussion of this topic on the program of the 1961 meeting indicates the importance of the issues it raised. Gardner gave several reasons for judging the election of the first Roman Catholic to the White House to be a most significant event, and suggested how it revealed the complexity of voting patterns in America and the diversity of religious influence on those patterns. Bryan, less sure Kennedy's success signaled a permanent victory for religious tolerance, described some of the hate mail that had been distributed during the campaign and indicated grave doubts that the antagonisms it revealed would be quickly dissipated from our national life. He decried the great silence of many Protestant leaders, who should have been offering light to counter the hate. Maston, surveying the teaching of pre-*aggiornamento* Roman Catholicism on church/state issues, wondered whether the presence of a Catholic layman in the White House would lead the Catholic hierarchy to modify the traditional rhetoric about the the duty of those possessing the "truth" to determine policy irrespective of popular will. Turnbull noted how quickly the issues that were felt so acutely during the campaign had ceased to agitate the public once the choice was made, and saw the results to involve a secularizing of the political realm in a way that would make a candidate's religious affiliation less and less a divisive factor in forthcoming campaigns. Forell reported on reactions among people in the Lutheran Church, in which there had been some isolated instances of blatant bigotry during the campaign. He also commented on a statement issued by twenty Lutheran theological school professors declaring that to vote against a candidate solely because of his religious affiliation would be a breach of the tradition of separation of church and state.

Except for this panel there is a noteworthy paucity of papers dealing directly with political themes all through the 1960s. The Society did not pick up the interest in political theology that was increasingly manifest in Europe during the late 1960s and early 1970s. No paper given at any of its programs used the phrase "political theology" --a phrase that was beginning to be widely used in Europe-- though by 1974 we do find a session announced with the title: "Biblical Politics and the Transfiguration of Revolution." This was the occasion at which Paul Lehmann's forthcoming book, *The Transfiguration of Politics* (Harper and Row, 1975), was discussed at a Sunday morning plenary session. Parts of Lehmann's book had been reproduced and distributed to members attending the meeting, and even more of the book had been made available to three members of the Society acting as panelists. Because that portion of the manuscript distributed on the general basis contained only limited clues to the argument as a whole, one of the designated respondents, Edward L. Long, Jr., provided an overview of the book at the beginning of the session. Then, the other respondents, Charles E. Curran and Bruce Morgan, gave more analytical critiques, and Long also posed questions to Lehmann. Long's brief synopsis of the argument, the critiques by Curran and Morgan, and the questions formulated by Long were included in the mimeographed materials distributed to the entire Society after the meeting.

Lehmann had developed a highly dialectical treatment of revolutionary politics which defended the legitimacy of revolution while at the same time indicating that the Christian faith must save revolutions from their own undoing. In contrast to many political theologies of the time that were focusing on eschatology as the locus for defending revolutionary change, Lehmann utilized the doctrine of the Incarnation for thinking about revolution. He also suggested that freedom is prior to order, reversing the traditional assertion that order is of primary importance. Lehmann strongly implied that all past revolutions had been unsatisfactory in one way or another. In the discussion that followed Charles Curran pressed Lehmann to show why using the Incarnation as the center of political thinking could render future revolutions less subject to undoing than have been past revolutions. He challenged Lehmann to be more articulate about the problem of means in revolutionary situations, particularly to spell out the criteria Lehmann would apply to determine when violence might be legitimate. In light of the record of laissez-faire capitalism, which puts a certain kind of freedom ahead of human need, Curran wanted further clarification of the contention that freedom is prior to order. Morgan drew a distinction between "ethics of casuistry, or measured calculation," and "ethics of inspiration, or prophetic vision." He characterized Lehmann's work as an impressive example of the latter, but wondered whether ethics of that sort can ever hope to answer the concerns that are important for ethics of the first sort. He also asked Lehmann to be more explicit in spelling out what his code words of "submission and silence, supplication and transfiguration" would actually mean to a person faced with violence as a moral problem. Long asked Lehmann to be more explicit in defining what he meant by revolution, and to give clearer indications of the role of the theological ethicist in making distinctions between revolutions that are transfiguring and those that are merely self-serving.

The presidential address in 1974 was given by Charles West and was entitled "Religion, Revolution and the Task of Ethics." West examined the relationship between secularization and religion on the one hand, and faith and ideology on the other. Making reference to the experience of Dietrich Bonhoeffer, West summarized the benefits that have come about when religious people have learned to recognize and support the service of humanity and justice from whatever sources it comes, whether or not identified with the proper metaphysical and ecclesiastical warrants. West then observed that this theological stance, despite its eloquent defense from thinkers like Harvey Cox, had given way before movements that were heavily ideological in character and went after their goals with all the vehemence of true believerism. "The poise and tension of secularized existence collapsed because it was understood, not as an expression of faith, not as a theological perception of faith, not as a theological perception in society, but as a humanistic proposition, as secularism. . ." West observed that Christian realism had produced people on both sides of the Vietnam conflict, those who had taken us step by step into the conflict and those who had opposed involvement with great vehemence. According to West, the fact that Christian realism had functioned ideologically to bolster particular political judgments rather than as an expression of an underlying faith caused it to lose the very theological power it could have exercised had it kept the affirmation of redeeming reality as central to its concerns as it had kept alive the principle of criticism and analysis. The other reason the theological vision of a secularized existence proved unable to carry the burden of the times was because civil religion, for all the values Bellah rightly saw in it, lacked the capacity to respond to a transcendent God. According to West these considerations make the question of faith crucial to the task of Christian ethics. West argued that the discipline of Christian ethics cannot be merely a descriptive enterprise that brackets the issue of faith. Only a revelatory encounter with a transcendent God who corrects both ideology and experience by forcing us to see the other human person in light of the ultimate Other (who is God at work among us) can save the Christian ethicist from the fate that has befallen so much of the contemporary religious world. There is something strangely similar between the arguments of Lehmann and those of West, though their analytical frameworks are so different that the similarity does not leap out and demand attention. Each was speaking of a kind of continuing transfiguration of existence that cannot be neglected if Chistians, or the political order of which they are a part, are to be made whole, and which cannot be worked out merely by balancing competing interests in a political process that has no central value commitments compatible to a Christian perspective.

The issues raised by West were pivotal, though perhaps they were so pivotal that they could not be dealt with adequately with the analytical tools that were by their very nature sources of the problem. Indeed, if the diagnosis West made was on target, then the very possibility of having a revelatory faith experience at the center of the ethical enterprise as commonly pursued is indeed remote. The task of realizing the kind of a world Bonhoeffer commended theologically as the locus of such an experienced reality is one which we generally are not equipped to handle.

But the issue, for all its complexities, would not go away. It has haunted the deliberations of the Society about political matters, even in papers that may not have been conscious of exploring it. Several papers or panels in subsequent years can be interpreted as exploring (probably unwittingly) the problem which West had identified. These presentations did not always agree with West. Sometimes they illustrated the very tendencies he had sought to delineate.

In 1975, one of the concurrent sessions consisted of a panel, composed of Alan B. Anderson, William S. Minor, and Douglas Sturm, which examined the relationship between "the Public Interest and Ultimate Commitment." Sturm's contribution to this panel is printed in *The Selected Papers*, and Anderson's is available in the archives. Minor furnished an outline of his talk and pointed to the relevance of his essay "The Public Interest and Ultimate Commitment," in Nomos V: The Public Interest, Carl J. Friedrich, ed. (Lieber-Atherton: 1962).

Anderson subtitled his part in the panel "A Semantic Analysis." He acknowledged the lack of any general agreement as to what is meant by the word "public" and the even greater uncertainty as to what is meant by "ultimate". Following a methodology appropriated from Richard McKeon, he looked at how the term "public" is used in four contemporary works: Walter Lippman's *The Public Philosophy*; Hannah Arendt's *The Human Condition*; Edwin C. Banfield's and James Q. Wilson's *City Politics*; and John Dewey's *The Public and Its Problems*. His presentation clearly documented the fundamental differences. In his paper Sturm acknowledged the fact that the term "public interest" has long been devoid of any substantial meaning. He noted how Cicero could speak of the public good or the interest of the people because public life was felt to be grounded in right reason and true law. But the meaning of the term that Cicero cherished has long since been obliterated in modern Western industrial society. Also referring to both Lippman and Dewey, Sturm asked how the notion of the "public interest" is to be recaptured. Outlining a complex set of interrelationhips between various levels of public identity, diverse interests that need to be considered, and different foci of concerns that have to be borne in mind, Sturm contended that at this juncture the procedural task of facilitating communication may be the greatest challenge we face.

The concern for the meaning of public purpose and the necessity to understand the nature of our common life was canvassed in the opening plenary of the 1976 meeting. Richard John Neuhaus was asked to address the Society on the title, "The Prospect of Democracy." Neuhaus suggested that the prospects for liberal democracy are not good because it faces a crisis of meaning. A few months later he published an article entitled "Democratic Prospect," in *Worldview* 19 (July to August 1976): 13-20. In that article he observed that many nations of the world are calling themselves democracies, but that constitutional democracies which cherish "liberal" ideas deserve religious and ideological support. Neuhaus has subsequently become increasingly prominent in calling attention to the value of democratic freedom as an arena for working out a sense of American purpose.

In another concurrent session in 1975, Richard Taylor, of The Movement for a New Society, described the commitments and the agenda of that group. Clues to the approach of the group, which has an intentional agenda, may be found in "Peace Makers: Faith and Obedience through Non-violent

Direct Action," *Post American [Sojourners]* 4 (October to November 1975): 16-21. The contrast between the presentations in the panel with Anderson, Sturm, and Minor, the plenary by Neuhaus, and the presentation by Taylor show how quickly the church/sect (or the culture-embracing vs. culture-rejecting) dichotomy will appear whenever the political question becomes a matter of theological scrutiny.

Since 1975 there have been only three papers dealing with political issues in a direct or theoretical manner. In 1978 George A. Chauncey announced for the program: "Influencing Public Policy: A Case study," but the paper was more accurately titled (as it is on a written version): "Theological Reflections on an Ecumenical Effort to Influence Public Policy." Chauncey gave an account of the work of the Interreligious Task Force on U. S. Food Policy, which he had a key role in organizing and which he chaired. This was a group brought together by the staffs of some twenty national religious groups having Washington offices. Its purpose was to create a joint witness on the problem of world hunger. Chauncey's paper, which assesses both the accomplishments and failures of the task force, outlines the lessons which he learned from this undertaking. Chauncey saw the work of the group as highly successful when judged as an ecumenical venture, exceedingly diligent in its preparation of policy recommendations, and well respected by policy-makers. But he noted the inability of the task force to mobilize grass-roots support from the sponsoring constituencies, and the difficulties (if not impossibilities) of a largely voluntary association mastering the technical competence needed to produce an outstanding level of inquiry and analysis of the issues. Chauncey urged the members of the Society to become more concerned with the ways in which their technical competence can be brought to bear on the decision-making processes in our government.

Returning to the historical roots of our political heritage, Robin Lovins presented a paper at the 1979 meeting on "Natural Law and Popular Sovereignty: The Constitutional Theory of James Wilson (1742-1798)". Wilson, though lesser known than Jefferson or Madison, was an important founding father of the United States, and in addition to participating in the drawing up of the Constitution, served on the Supreme Court after the new government was established. Wilson, something of an American Blackstone, was possibly the most learned of his contemporaries and joined belief in a theory of natural law with a commitment to popular sovereignty. It is this latter factor that intrigued Lovins. Wilson was able to bring together two ideas that are often regarded as in tension, if not indeed as irreconcilable, because his Scottish training in the "moral common sense" theories that were then in vogue made it possible for him to believe that the people would cherish a moral right and thus provide a reliable safeguard against "every distemper of government."

It is somewhat surprising to see how many of the papers dealing with political thought have been intrigued by the notion of "peoplehood" or the "public" consciousness. This has interested more presenters of papers as the crucial factor in politics than has the nature of power, and was the focus of a paper given by William W. Everett in 1982 with the title "Toward God's Perfect Public." Suggesting that the symbol of the Kingdom of God has lost its appeal because the monarchical model is no longer normative (even for many authoritarian regimes) Everett examined the possibilities in the symbol of God's Republic. The paper moves through a wide range of theological reflection--from the Bible and Augustine to Rauschenbusch, Reinhold Niebuhr, and contemporary writers to suggest the plausibility of using the idea of a republic in place of the idea of a kingdom to symbolize the nature of Christian corporate existence. In this concept the ideal of the public is important. It is an idea that transcends the individualism of much existential thought yet does not relegate all significance to the political or economic structures of state or corporation. Everett delved rather extensively into personality theory as well as political theory in developing an understanding of salvation as the struggle for public viability.

Thinking About the Nature of Law

The subject of law has received considerable attention in the programs of the Society. Perhaps this is because several of its members have engaged in the special study of law as a way of extending their conceptual horizons. Perhaps it is because a few teachers of law have been closely associated with the Society. Perhaps it is because the subject of law is inherently more conservative in its implications that the subject of politics. More likely it is because a Task Force on Religion and Law actively promoted the discussion of the relationships between these two kinds of learning and professional activity.

Except for one paper by Dean M. Kelley, given in 1964 on the subject "Differentiation of Church and State: Inhibition or Enablement," all of the sessions dealing with law have been on the programs of the Society in the last half of its history. The programs that were planned by the Task Force on the Harrisburg Conspiracy Trials in 1972 (see chapter three) were the first of a whole series of presentations dealing with legal matters. In 1975, Robert C. L. Moffat looked at the problems related to "The Legal Enforcement of

Morality." He considered the debate that had raged for many years between Patrick Devlin and H. L. A. Hart about the legal enforcement of morals and cited several philosophical and legal writers whose thinking was significant for understanding the issues posed by that debate.

In 1974, James Childress studied "Appeals to Conscience in Moral, Religious and Legal Discourse". Published in *Ethics* 89 (July 1979): 315-335, this paper concentrates on the problems created when individuals invoke their own consciences to justify conduct that is not in keeping with normal mores or legal standards. Childress argued that we should start with the presumption of liberty of conscience, and require the state to bear the burden of proof that its interests are so overriding as to make it important to deny the right of the individual to act or refuse to act on the basis of that individual's private judgment as to the moral good. In 1977, Leslie Rothenberg's paper, given at the meeting as "Law, Ethics, and Theology," but published in *The Selected Papers* as "The Role of Judges and the Courts as Definers of Ethical Values," used three different court cases to show how judges are increasingly assuming a role in making ethical norms. His extensive comments about the Karen Ann Quinlan case are a contribution to biomedical ethics as well as to thinking about the relationship between religion and law. The 1977 meeting also had a panel on "Law and Ethics." Frederick Carney, and two guests, Justice Patrick Hart, and Dean Thomas Shaffer participated, but like the substance of so many panels the content was not preserved in written form.

Considerable attention was paid to issues of religion and law in 1979, and members of the Society who wished to do so could hear a number of papers on this topic. Immediately before the regular meeting of the Society, a conference on "Legal and Ethical Dimensions of Religious Freedom" was sponsored by the Institute of Social Ethics, an agency of the School of Religion and the Center for the Humanities of the University of Southern California. The conference, not officially conducted by the Society, featured addresses by Harold Berman and Alan Dershowitz of Harvard Law School, Richard Delgado of the University of Washington Law School, Austin Straus of Amnesty International, and Hillel Levine of Yale University. The regular program of the Society had four papers dealing with the relationship of Religion and Law, two (to be noted below) addressed specific issues. Raymond Decker, Director of Research, Development, and Planning of the Archdiocese of San Francisco, who had just spent a year at the Harvard Law School examining religious presuppositions of criminal law, agreed to address a panel sponsored by the Task Force on Religion and Law on the topic

"Crime As Sin: Religious Assumptions in Criminal Law." Decker tried to find some congruity between sin and crime by suggesting that both are in some way disorderly and intentional. He argued that the development of American criminal law has been heavily influenced by Christian ethical doctrine; he indicated that the acknowledgement of subjective liability in American law gives it common ground with Christian teaching; and he contended that the understanding of punishment as (at least in part) retribution makes American civil law closer to a natural law than to a positivist orientation. In responding, Douglas Sturm acknowledged some validity to these points but felt that stringent qualifications were necessary in order not to destroy important distinctions between crime and sin. Leslie Rothenberg also responded to the paper, but his remarks are not found in the archives. In another paper at the 1979 meeting, R. Kenneth Manning, Jr. looked at a line of appellate cases, including several from the United States Supreme Court, in which natural law reasoning had been operative. The paper is published in *The Selected Papers* under the title "Due Process and Individual Rights in Court Decisions on Property and Liberty." In 1980 John Langan gave a paper on "Punishment and Morality in Thomas Aquinas."

In addition to the papers dealing with broad foundational issues concerning law and religion, a number of papers given since 1978 have examined a particular social issue or problem in connection with which legal considerations are pivotally important. Except for 1981, every year from 1978 to 1983 there have been at least two, and sometimes three, papers prsented on the subject of law. In 1978 L. Harold Dewolf, participating with Joseph Fletcher in a panel on "Continuity and Change in Ethics," looked at the Criminal Justice system. The same year, Barbara and Alan Andolsen directed attention toward "Privacy, Confidentiality, and Information Systems." Taking note of the increasing rate at which information is gathered about individuals in modern society, the Andolsens contended that present laws are inadequate to protect individuals against abuse. They enunciated certain procedures that should be observed to guard the rights of individuals and proposed certain checks to be placed on the methods by which data are gathered. Warren Copeland examined "The Ethics of Welfare Reform," looking at specific proposals for improving the system and citing six criteria for an adequate welfare program. His paper was published in *The Selected Papers* for 1978, but even before it appeared in that form it was published as an article in *The Christian Century 95* (May 31, 1978): 580-581, with the title "Welfare Reform and Social Change."

Two papers were included in the program for 1979 that

dealt with specific applications of the law in the social process. Edward A. Malloy considered the problems involved in police work, particularly the possibility that law enforcement officers may have to employ violence. In "Ethics and Police Intervention in Domestic Violence," he indicated the wide discretionary powers that lower eschelon law enforcement officers frequently have in deciding when and under what conditions to employ their fire arms, and presented sixteen propositions drawn to a large extent from a modification of just war teaching--for deciding which uses of force are morally appropriate. The paper urged a serious and intensive effort to achieve a professional image of police work as rapidly as possible. William W. Everett presented a paper entitled "Land Ethics," which developed a systematic account of issues that should be taken into account in determining land use. This paper is printed in *The Selected Papers*.

In 1980 James F. Smurl examined the extent to which there is "A Right to Legal Services," and Glen Stassen discussed "Issues in the Death Penalty Debate." According to Smurl's paper, although the Constitution affirms the right of every accused person to competent legal counsel, this principle was given only lip service in America until 1963, when the Supreme Court gave explicit definition for implementing it. Commenting on the significance of this great gap between ideals and practice, Smurl emphasized the need for legal ethics to take structured conditions into account, not merely the good will or personal qualities of lawyers. He also argued the necessity of grounding legal ethics in humanistic and not merely scientific considerations, and the importance of challenging and not merely accommodating to existing cultural mores. Stassen's paper, which was printed in *The Annual*, was an autobiographical account of his role in presenting testimony before Kentucky juries in death penalty cases--testimony that seems to have been effective in persuading juries not to demand the supreme penalty.

In 1982 Richard H. Hiers delivered a paper on "Title VII and Judicial Policy-Making 1971-81," a comprehensive analysis of efforts to end racial and gender based discrimination in employment under the Civil Rights Act of 1964. Hiers concluded that by and large courts have been quicker to recognize and correct violations based on racial than on sexual discrimination. This paper appeared a year after it was delivered in the Professional Resource Section of *The Annual* for 1983. In 1982 Edward Malloy did a paper on "The Isolation of the Criminal Agent: The Christian Rationale for Imprisonment." Malloy reviewed the main theories of criminal punishment (the retributive temperament, the general deterrence rationale, the rehabilitative perspective, and the isolating, or "special deterrence" view) and argued that the last could be most satisfactorily reconciled with a Christian perspective. Only criminals who threaten the common good because of demonstrated tendencies for impulsive and predatory aggression need to be imprisoned (that is, isolated from society for the protection of society). The third paper in 1982, given by Janet Dickey McDowell, was entitled "The Ethical Foundation of Bilingual Education Law." This paper examined the 1974 Supreme Court decision, Lau v. Nichols, which gave the force of law to regulations of the Department of Health, Education, and Welfare requiring school districts to provide special programs for pupils deficient in English because of their backgrounds. Such programs were designed to make the benefits of general instruction more equally available to all pupils. The decision is based on a welfare rather than a just due concept of equality and, according to McDowell, is thoroughly consistent with Christian ethical understandings of justice. The paper indicated at the end how the administrative policies of the Reagan administration have undercut the significance of this decision.

The considerable diversity in the topics covered under the rubric of law indicates how many ethically important issues are touched upon by the function of law. The future will probably find many more issues dealt with under this rubric.

Treatment of Human Rights

The subject of human rights has been discussed in papers given before the Society nine times, but all nine of these times have been in the last six years of the Society's history. In 1978 the opening plenary session was devoted to a discussion of human rights. William P. Thompson, Stated Clerk of the United Presbyterian Church in the USA, and Congressman Robert Drinan of Massachusetts were guests of the Society to present this theme in an opening plenary session. Herbert Richardson was scheduled to give a paper on "Human and Civil Rights in the 'New Religion'" but was not able to attend the meeting. The next year John Pawlikowski gave a paper on "Human Rights in the Catholic Tradition." The paper, published in *The Selected Papers*, gave a historical account of Roman Catholic teaching and examined some contemporary efforts to come forth with an adequate formulation on this issue. At the same meeting Aurelia Rule discussed "Human Rights: Aspects and Questions," and Richard Roach, "Theology and Ethics in Human Rights Arguments."

In 1980 George R. Lucas, Jr. examined "The Inviolability Principle: Human Needs and Human Rights." Lucas pointed to the fundamental difference between a libertarian tradition that thinks of human rights primarily as guarantees against governmental interference in personal lives, and those perspectives that look at human rights in terms of the fair allocation of resources insuring the survival and well-being of each member of society. The first of these views might be said to tolerate ghettos as the price of freedom while the second, to tolerate gulags in order to pursue economic planning that attempts to care for all. According to Lucas, the best contemporary thinking about human rights seeks to avoid this sharp dichotomy and speaks about "the right to have vital needs fulfilled at the same time as freedom is cherished." Acknowledging that "needs" cannot always be equivalent to "rights," the paper sought to develop an adequate theological concept of how these two ideas are related. The overriding consideration is that the humanity of persons not be violated, a consideration Lucas found alive in the early writing of Karl Marx and the contemporary writing of the Czech theologian Milan Machovec, as well as in thinkers in the libertarian tradition. The inviolability principle precludes both the infringement of thought or speech and the deprivation of essential needs such as food, education, and health care and requires societies to be concerned about both. This paper was published in *Encounter* 45 (Winter 1984): 1-10. On at least two occasions Lucas has also provided members of the Society attending the annual meeting with copies of excellent bibliographies on human rights issues.

In 1982 Ronald Stone looked at the relationship between "Christian Realism and Human Rights." Stone has been working hard to distance Christian realism from the "realpolitik" and reductionistic militarism so rampant in recent years. In this paper he was critical of tendencies to use human rights only as an ideological factor in a cold war. His paper showed how much the thinking of Reinhold Niebuhr has affected both sides in some of the debates. It provided a careful and detailed analysis of the hearings before the Senate Foreign Relations Committee on the nomination of Ernest E. Lefever to head the Human Rights Division of the U. S. Department of State. Those hearings brought to light sharply divergent views about the human rights question even among those holding a realist position.

The twenty-fourth annual meeting of the Society in 1983 had two papers dealing with human rights issues. One was given by John Langan on the subject: "Roman Catholic Theological Anthropology as a Basis for Human Rights." Langan outlined the current conversation as to whether the advocacy of human rights requires a grounding in theological anthropology--as Max Stackhouse has argued in a chapter on this issue in a book edited by Alfred Hennelly and John Langan

(*Human Rights in the Americas: The Struggle for Consensus*, Georgetown University Press, 1982). Langan contended that Roman Catholicism has come to an appropriate position on human rights more from historical experience than from a logical unfolding of the implications of a theological anthropology--a fact that makes it difficult to hold that theological reflection about human nature is the main, if not sole, source of this social concern. But Langan also recognized that theological anthropology has a contribution to make in understanding human rights. Consequently, "Christians need both to ground human rights norms in their own theology and to acknowledge the positive contribution of non-Christian and non-religious individuals, movements, and institutions in formulating, applying, and defending human rights norms against the excesses of inhumanity which mark the troubled progress of humanity." The other 1983 paper, by James Will, looked at "Church and Theology in the Struggle for Human Rights in Poland." Drawing on the insights of Paul Tillich about social conditions under tyranny, it examined the political and economic power of Marxism in Poland, the rise of groups like Solidarity, and the role of the Church in relation to attempts of Polish society to solve its economic problems.

There is an instructive contrast between the theoretical considerations presented in Langan's paper and the historical and descriptive account of an actual situation in the paper by Will. One paper got to experience by raising a theoretical question and the other got to theory by looking at a historical situation. Perhaps that very contrast is a clue to the nature of Christian ethics and the uniqueness of the Society in holding together two very necessary aspects of a momentous task.

9

Economics, Technology and Vocational Ethics

All of the presentations to be considered in this chapter are concerned with how the pursuit or provision of goods and services affects the human condition. The first set of papers to be discussed concerns economic matters; the second, technology and the problems it poses; the third, ethical issues that arise while earning a living or engaging in a professional career.

Economics

While the Society opened its very first meeting with a panel on "A Christian Ethic for an Affluent Society," (see chapter one), it was eight years before the program again focused attention on the ethical issues related to economic policy. But a topic long left untouched would then get attention from several directions. A session with Senator Eugene McCarthy had been scheduled in 1967 on the topic, "Some Aspects of Ethics in Government." When McCarthy was unable to keep the commitment, President Victor Obenhaus was able to get Frank McCollough of the National Labor Relations Board to substitute. Another session that same year featured Hyman H. Bookbinder, Assistant Director of the Office of Economic Opportunity, who spoke on the "Ethical Philosophy of the Poverty Program." Shortly after speaking to the Society, Bookbinder jointly authored (with Lorald K. Shulz), "Lovers' Quarrel Over the Poverty Program," *The Christian Century* 27 (July 24, 1967): 177-79.

The presidential address for 1967, given by Victor Obenhaus, was on "The Ethics of Income Distribution." Obenhaus noted that while much attention was then being given to the amelioration of poverty, relatively little was being devoted to the closely related, but distinctively different, problem of income distribution. The address was laced with statistics concerning the patterns of income that prevailed at the time, and reviewed the provisions of various plans, both private and public, that were being suggested to alleviate the plight of those without sufficient income.

Considering the ethical issues, Obenhaus contended that the main obstacles to lifting the burden of poverty from the lowest 20% of the population were not financial, but philosophical, sociological, and even theological. Noting that a country where neighbors once rather routinely got together for barn raisings does have a heritage of mutual aid as well as of private entrepreneuralism, Obenhaus argued that there is no reason why that concept of mutual aid cannot be legitimized in new ways, so that every citizen of our society is cared for. Any scheme for doing this, Obenhaus observed, would need to take the problem of incentives into account as well as the principle that no one in an affluent society should starve. Obenhaus asserted that "a society capable of technological 'miracles' can resolve the dilemma of inequality and make dignity available to all."

Economic issues reappeared on the program in 1971, and again they would be addressed in more than just one session. In one presentation Richard Dickinson, Jr. looked at "World Economic Development and the Question of Justice" and Norman Faramelli, at "Structural Economic Power in America: An Ethical Critique." According to Dickinson we lack the basic technical knowledge of how best to promote development (not merely the political will to do so); we should not think of world development in merely economic terms or expect Western technological models to be adequate for achieving it; and we need a global and systemic strategy to grasp the problem vigorously. Dickinson also declared that uncontrolled private enterprise cannot produce justice. He called on seminary faculties to prepare themselves in the technical aspects of economics so they can provide a credible witness about these issues. Faramelli's paper focused on the economic and political power of large American corporations and the ethical issues raised by that power. He showed how pervasively the tax system favors the rich, how the government provides subsidies for large economic undertakings, and how the concentration of wealth has remained fairly constant since 1929. He cited the dominance of two huge forces--the military industrial complex and the highway industrial complex and set down four principles by which economic policy should be governed: 1) individual freedom and community self-determination should be enhanced; 2) trends toward economic equality must increase; 3) technical achievements must respect the laws of the natural order; and 4) a genuine pluralism of economic forces should be developed. He suggested several steps for coping with corporate power, including improved regulation, the creation of private technical institutes to protect the consumer, and the devising of new kinds of community organizations to monitor these problems. He pled with Christian ethicists to recapture the concern for economic justice that once characterized ecumenical bodies.

The other part of the 1971 program devoted to economic issues was the Sunday morning plenary session, which was on the topic, "National Priorities: Who Should Get What, How, and Why?" This period was devoted to a critical evaluation of the papers at the previous sessions and Peter Paris launched a general discussion by suggesting that it is important to begin with concrete practice and move to theoretical considerations in dealing with these issues.

The discussion of economic questions as a problem of national policy would return to the programs of the Society in six years, when the problem of poverty would again be in the forefront of discussion. The few papers presented in the interval between 1971 and 1977 examined certain other issues that bear on how people are affected by economic conditions. In 1973 Donald W. Shriver, Jr. gave a paper entitled "Millhands and Preachers Revisited: Ethics and Ideology in a Southern Mill Community." This paper shared with members of the Society the findings of work then in progress toward the publication in 1976 of *Spindles and Spires* co-authored with John R. Earle and Dean D. Knudson and published by John Knox Press, 1976. In 1974 there was a paper by Keith Bridston with the title: "Wilson Distributors: A Case Study in Ethics." Bridston's paper examined a Harvard Business School case of a trucking firm having trouble with pilfering. The owners regarded the matter as theft; the drivers as a fringe benefit. Bridston showed from this case how perceptions of things differ depending upon the perspective from which they are seen. This paper was more concerned with exploring the problems in teaching ethics than with the economic issues involved. Bridston was at the time publishing articles about the case method way of teaching ethics. One of these appeared as "Case Study in Teaching Theology," *Atlanta Theological Library Association: Proceedings* (1973): 71 4; and the other as "Metaphysics of the Mundane: The Theological Implications of the Case Study Method," *Theological Education* 10 (Spring, 1974): 139-52.

A paper by Ronald Stone given in 1976 examined the thought of Paul Tillich on both economic and political affairs. Stone, aware that some scholars were suggesting that Tillich abandoned his socialist vision in later years to settle for belief in a dispersion of power in a mixed economy, contended that the vision of religious socialism remained an essential ingredient in Tillich's thinking all through his life. Stone showed that many of the ideas Tillich advanced were very similar to outlooks being currently advanced by political and liberation theologies.

Shortly after giving this paper Stone published two articles on the subject: "Tillich: Radical Political Theologian," *Religion in Life* 46 (September 1977): 44-53; and "Tillich's Critical Use of Marx and Freud in the Social Context of the Frankfort School," *Union Seminary Quarterly Review* 83 (Fall 1977): 3-9.

In 1976 Henry B. Clark II gave a paper "Pressure for Change: Ethical Reflections on American Life Style." *The Selected Papers* for that same year also contain a paper that was originally delivered before the meeting of the West Coast Section of the Society by Donald E. Miller: "Life Style: A Category for the Analysis of Moral Identity." Miller's paper covered a broad range of issues concerning how Christian social ethics ought to be done. It suggested that the ways in which people work, eat, worship, entertain, consume, and recreate provide a distinctive way of learning "what is going on" in a given situation. "The ethicist's role," argued Miller," is to clarify varying patterns of value commitments by depicting and analyzing the life styles that predominate in the community being studied."

In 1977 papers dealing with public policy aspect of economic issues reappear on the Society's program. Unfortunately a goodly number of these papers were given by guests or have not been obtainable for the record. Gregory Baum gave a paper at the opening plenary session entitled "Democracy and Capitalism: Canadian and Theological Perspectives." John Dillon discussed "The Struggle for a More Just Trade Policy." James F. Smurl looked at "Debates About Poverty: Henry George's Response to Pope Leo XIII." This historical exploration entitled, "Ethics and Culture: An Historical Instance with Theoretical and Practical Implications," focused on the way in which Henry George responded to Pope Leo XIII's encyclical *Rerum Novarum* (On the Conditions of Labor). George, a religious socialist, felt that the encyclical attacked his single tax movement and its underlying philosophy, and he also felt that while Leo verbally rejected socialism, he also had embraced much of its underlying approach. Smurl suggested that George intended his tract to be read by an American audience that was hostile to claims of distributive justice but he also indicated that George felt Americans were repelled as much or more by complex argument as by the basic premises of distributive justice. Smurl suggested that ethicists must be more concerned, along with other humanists, with the ways in which moral arguments impact those whose response patterns are shaped by cultural outlooks. Prevailing mores often preclude serious and rigorous attention to moral principles.

This same year, in a paper on "The Ethics of Entitlement," Major J. Jones raised many issues involving economic justice, the significance of work, the difficulties of charity, and the problems of welfare. He took note of the rising feeling that people are entitled to a decent standard of living simply because they are human, and noted that this creates a quite different premise than does a welfare system. The one stresses rights; the other, charity. A shift to the idea of entitlement can, in turn, produce contempt and condescending disdain among the privileged, who believe that the right to an acceptably decent livlihood is earned, not guaranteed. But, Jones indicated, the bulk of welfare goes to people who for a variety of reasons cannot work. Among the poor in general there is a latent incentive to work, though as the assumption of entitlement gets strong, this incentive can give way to a feeling that it is acceptable to use assertive techniques to insure that one gets that to which one is entitled. For instance, the looters who rampaged through the city during the New York blackout revealed how quite a few persons were ready to commit crimes in order to obtain that to which they thought themselves entitled. Alas, the privileged also assume, on a quite different level, that they are entitled to certain privileges and immunities--for instance, the right to leave the less fortunate behind in the scramble for success.

Jones then sought to balance the idea of legitimate entitlement with the traditional moral repudiation of greed, and asked how far and to what extent the natural right to an adequate standard of living can be carried. He suggested that the Western work ethic, which has dominated thinking about these matters for a long time, is threatened, and noted how many persons on the margins of society find it more tempting to resort to crime, or to a street existence that turns a legal but largely unearned buck, than to submit to the depersonalizing and relatively unrewarding kinds of work offered to so many on the bottom of the productive ladder. This underclass lives by using the same cunning at the bottom of the economic scale as does the upperclass at the top. Jones indicated that great difficulties face a culture in which these changes in value commitments are taking place on a wide scale and at a rapid rate.

In 1979 Prentiss Pemberton delivered a paper on "Justice and Efficiency in a Christian Economic Ethic." Daniel Finn responded. This paper is not available, but Pemberton and Finn are working on a book on economic justice that will probably develop the ideas explored at this session.

Attention to economic justice picks up considerably in the programs during the 1980s. The first year of the new decade saw three sessions devoted to this issue. One of these, entitled "Is America Fair? Ethics and Current

Economic Prospects," was presented as the opening plenary session. Robert Lekachman of Lehmann College and Harvey H. Segal of Citibank gave different responses to the question. Segal later published "Economics for People: Hope on a Far Horizon," in *Christianity and Crisis* 40 (September 29, 1980): 257-261. The same year Daniel R. Finn delivered a paper on "The Ethical Orientation of Schools of Economic Thought." This was published in *The Annual*, but in the year 1982 rather than the year in which the paper was given. Finn outlined the ethical orientation of six of the seven major schools of economic thought and suggested that this may provide an opening for the needed dialogue between economists and ethicists.

Another 1980 paper, originally given by Normand J. Paulhaus with the title "The Fribourg Union and Social Catholicism," was published in *The Selected Papers* with the revised title "Social Catholicism and the Fribourg Union." This paper gave a historical account of the yearly meetings of the group and its basic social teaching. While opposed to socialism, this relatively small gathering was adamant in its advocacy of social justice, and did much to address the economic problems of the late nineteenth century. The Fribourg movement in Europe was contemporaneous with the efforts of Francis Greenwood Peabody and others in America to address the social question. Finn's paper examines the efforts of this group to hammer out doctrinal positions on matters such as just compensation, state interference in economic processes, the proper significance of private property, the banking system, workers' insurance, and the concept of the "corporative ideal." According to Finn, although the views of the Fribourg Union have been considered outdated and sterile, they may indeed yet prove to be more prophetic than has been realized.

In 1981 the opening plenary session on Friday afternoon was devoted to a panel discussion on "Ecology, Energy, and Equality: Distributive Justice in a Time of Diminishing Resources." (A further discussion of this panel will come in the section of this chapter on technology). At this same meeting Jon P. Gunnemann gave a paper on "Ethics, Markets, and Theodicy." In his paper Gunnemann showed how free market thinking is used as a means of legitimizing a difference between private and public behavior postulated in "the axiom of the social paradox." This axiom is found in different ways in the economic thinking of Adam Smith, Albert Hirschman, Robert Malthus, and others, and in the political thinking of such different figures as Niccolo Machiavelli and Reinhold Niebuhr. The thought of these very different figures has served in quite different ways to differentiate between individual moral obligations and the behavior considered appropriate or functional between larger social groups. In a sense, "the paradox of the social axiom" becomes a kind of theodicy that is used to justify the evils that persist in the social order as the necessary condition for achieving a higher good. Gunnemann did not call for the paradox to be lightly dismissed, but he did suggest the importance of taking the classical ideals more seriously than is done when the social paradox is accepted too easily and uncritically as the starting point of analysis. This paper indicates the ingredients for an analysis of economic issues that is as insightful as the analysis that Gunnemann has made of political questions in his book *The Moral Meaning of Revolution* (Yale, 1979), and perhaps someday it will be made more generally available for us. John Raines, who responded a year later to Gunnemann's paper, gave his own presentation on "Economics and the Justification of Sorrows: A Critique of Free Market Ideology." The thrust of Raines's paper was to push more forcefully toward a concern about economic justice. In yet another paper in 1982 Jerome Kurtz discussed "The Social Impact of American Tax Legislation."

In 1983 the second plenary session in three years to be devoted to economic issues was held on Sunday morning, with William Tabb of Queens College giving an address on "The Social, Political, and Ethical Meaning of the 'Reagan Revolution.'" Tabb noted that Reaganomics is built on the theory that the liberty of the market place is to be exalted above collectivistic paternalism, but conceded that it might be little more than a raw power play threatening to divide the nation along income lines and to produce class conflict. Tabb also indicated how the whole Reagan approach appeals to a faith. It asks the nation to trust it will work prior to showing results, and to sustain its commitment even in face of evidence that it is not working. Another analysis of Reagan's economic policies was given at the same meeting by Warren Copeland in a paper entitled "The Economic Policy Debate and Sturm's Prism of Justice." Copeland suggested that the United States now had a truly ideological president, whose policies were based upon a consistent application of a fundamental philosophy of government. He charged that ethicists are unable to respond to the Reagan challenge with a reasoned critique because they have too long neglected the social question and those concerns for elementary economic justice that furnished the main impetus for the discipline. He commended Wogaman's *The Great Economic Debate* (Westminster Press, 1977) as furnishing the right criteria for evaluating economic programs, and transposed Sturm's prism of justice so as to apply it to economic rather than to political alternatives. He argued that ethicists must deal with economic issues by focusing attention on the need for equality and community--factors too often neglected when the only concern is upon freedom.

A discipline with the heritage of Rauschenbusch, Niebuhr, and a host of others having a great concern for economic justice, should look at this series of papers soberly. At the beginning of the Society's life some members were overly confident that a commitment to social justice was a well-established aspect of the national ethos, and that the main task was to implement that commitment more wisely and fully. Meanwhile a frontal challenge to that basic commitment has been mounted, and the result is that, in company with many others, the Society now finds itself "reactive" to almost revolutionary transitions that are transposing the economic and social realms into places for the free reign of Social Darwinism. Perhaps the most important papers of those given during the period just examined will turn out to be those which have looked at historical efforts to face social questions under conditions of severe economic injustice. By providing insight into how this was done in the past we may learn how it has to be redone in the present.

Technology and Society

Over the years some sixteen items on programs of the Society have been devoted to discussions of the impact of science and technology on the human condition. These discussions encompass a rather wide range of issues. Only one of these papers was given in the first twelve years of the Society's existence and ten of them were given in the last six years.

In 1963 Robert Batchelder looked at "Some Issues Confronting an Automated Society." Taking note of the simultaneous increase in technological automation and the growth of hard-core unemployment, Batchelder suggested that while there is considerable disagreement on whether automation produces a net loss of jobs, it is clear that those who are replaced by automation are frequently the unskilled who work at the bottom of the pay and status scales, while whatever new jobs are created are those demanding high skills. The result is that automation exacerbates the problem of hard-core unemployment among minorities and teenagers. Considering several proposed solutions to this problem, his paper indicated how difficult it is to get a consensus for the elimination of unemployment in a nation that rather quickly agrees on goals such as defeating Hitler, beating the Russians to the moon, or building an interstate highway system.

There were four papers on technology given before the society in the early 1970s. In 1971 James E. Allen and

L. Harold DeWolf shared a session entitled "Population, Environment, and Ideology." Allen's paper argued, from the facts then generally held be true, that the United States (as other parts of the world) has a population problem brought about largely by the enthusiasm for reproduction found in middle class families, and that we must make two rather than three children the norm for the average American family. Allen explored various suggestions for accomplishing this result and asked to what extent we would be warranted in restricting individual liberties in order to curtail the population boom. DeWolf, indicating with many detailed illustrations the extent of the pollution problem, suggested that the ecological crisis, although threatening disaster only if unchecked, provides an unprecedented opportunity to unite all races and ideologies in the pursuit of a common purpose, to turn our efforts away from materialistic endeavours, and to create a new partnership between science and religion.

In 1973 Jørgen Randers was invited to be the Society's guest at the opening plenary session. Prior to his appearance, a complimentary copy of his book, *The Limits of Growth*, was sent to every member of the Society by Rodney Shaw of the Methodist Board of Social Concern. Members were urged to read this document (popularly known as "The Club of Rome Report") before coming to the meeting, since Randers expected to confine his presentation to highlighting certain issues and then open the session to discussion. Norman Faramelli and Robert Stivers initiated this discussion by providing the first responses to Randers. Another paper was given in 1973 by Arthur J. Dyck on "Population and National Responsibility: An Ethical Analysis of the Report on the Commission on Population Growth and the American Future." Dyck characterized the report as an essentially moral document concerned with issues such as the quality of life, freedom, and social justice. He examined three different positions on the population question from which the report might be judged, and distanced himself from the abortion policy implied in it. Dyck later published two articles dealing with related issues: "Population, Abortion and Human Welfare," *Perkins School of Theology Journal* 27 (Fall 1973): 41-9; and, "Procreative Rights and Population Policy," *The Hastings Center Studies* 1 (1973): 74-2.

In 1976 Waldo Beach looked at the impact of technology in a paper: "The Wheel and the Cross: A Christian Response to the Technological Revolution." The title of this paper became the title of a book that Beach published in 1979 with John Knox Press. In the paper Beach showed how technology as a faith system extols efficiency and brackets questions of purpose. This leads people to think that it is legitimate to do whatever can be done rather than to ask what ought to be done. Only a moral norm symbolized by the cross can insure that questions are asked about the human consequences of technological achievements.

Beginning in 1977, two years before the World Council of Churches Conference on Faith, Science, and the Future was held at the Massachusettes Institute of Technology, the programs of the Society showed a marked increase in the number of papers dealing with scientific developments. Karl D. Hartzell delivered a paper on "Science and Valuation." Robert L. Stivers, having published his book *The Sustainable Society* (Westminster Press, 1976), gave a paper "The Sustainable Society: Realism and Hope," and several months later published an article, "The Sustainable Society: Religious and Social Implications, *Review of Religious Research* 21 (Fall 1979): 71-86. The year of the World Council Conference, Paul Abrecht, the staff member most closely involved in its planning, spoke to the Society on "Technology, Science and Values," and the year following the conference Roger Shinn and five other members of the Society who had attended (Paul Abrecht, Merle Longwood, Jane Cary Peck, Robert Stivers, and Preston Williams) presented a panel that looked at the accomplishments of the Conference.

Walter G. Muelder's presidential address in 1979, entitled "The Science of Limits and the Limits of Science," took direct note of the forthcoming World Council Conference, which Muelder saw as involving a tension between an endless striving after technical achievements and the limits that obviously must function if a society is to be "just, participatory, and sustainable." This address surveyed various efforts to develop a science of limits that was concerned with the conditions of organic and coherent growth in contrast to the mechanistic triumphalism and ruthless expansionism that have too often characterized the technological enterprise. It pointed out how both overdeveloped capitalism and technocratic communism fail to take adequate account of this science of limits, and are predatory and exploitative with respect to both nature and human potential. Examining in detail three studies--the Club of Rome's first report, its second report, and the United Nations's study of *The Future of the World Economy*, Muelder supported the point of view that people should participate in the decisions that affect their futures. But, he observed, this requires special social conditions and public skills. It requires a freedom in Christ to pursue the non-material aspects of life as well as the material ones. This address is found in *The Selected Papers*. A short while after giving this paper Muelder also published an article on closely related themes: "The New Debate on Faith, Science, and the

Future," *Andover Newton Theological Quarterly* 20 (March 1980): 199-207.

From 1978 to 1983 several presentations focused in one way or another on questions of energy. A panel in 1978 with Frederick Carney, Margaret Maxey, and Alvin Pitcher discussed "Ethical Aspects of the World Energy Crisis." Another panel in 1981 looked at "Ecology, Energy, and Equality: Distributive Justice in a Time of Diminishing Resources." This panel was given the plenary slot at the opening of the annual meeting and included as participants Wallace Ogg, Emeritus Professor of Economics at Iowa State University; Marty Strange, Director of the Center for Rural Affairs in Walthill, Nebraska; and Larry Rasmussen. In setting up this panel the planning committee hoped that the problem of providing energy, the problem of preserving the environment, and the problem of social justice--which are often discussed separately--might be considered in their interrelationships.

Other papers have dealt somewhat more generally with the impact of science on social behavior. Two were on the program in 1979. The first of these was a paper by Henry B. Clark and Donald Miller on "Energy Policy and Life Styles in California," and appears in *The Selected Papers 1979*. The second, by John T. Pawlikowski, examined "The Catholic Bishops' Statement on Energy: Its Implications for Public Ethics." Pawlikowski's paper was interesting, not only for its analysis of the content of the Bishops' statement, but for its description of the process that was used to formulate it. In fact, the planning committee had urged him to focus on the process more than upon the substance, for this statement was developed using the open hearing method and involving the resources of many groups, both Catholic and non Catholic. The process used to draw up this statement broke new procedural ground within the Roman Catholic Church and may well have been precedent setting for the more highly publicized Bishops' letter on nuclear weapons that was prepared subsequently. The bishops' letter on energy manifested a concern both for the care of persons and for the care of the earth. According to Pawlikowski, the document also moved to a more dynamic understanding of the relationship between the natural and human orders and may well have momentous implications for traditional natural law morality based upon more static understandings. It also called on Roman Catholics to accept some degree of limitation on their expectations, and modestly embraced the principle of subsidiarity as a strategy for dealing with energy issues. A third paper, presented in 1982 by Terence R. Anderson, dealt with "Ethics, Uranium Mining and Public Participation in Development Decisions: Canadian Perspectives on Ethics and Ecology." It was printed in the 1982 *Annual*.

It is interesting to note that in all this discussion of technology and related issues none of the papers has considered the space program or the landing of a human being on the moon, efforts into which the country was pouring enormous resources during those years and about which the public was intensely interested, albeit in an adventuresome rather than a moral way.

Issues Related to the Professions

The professions are a part of an economic/technological complex. All of the professions are involved in earning a living--and within narrow limits each of them codifies what practices are acceptable in that endeavour. To the extent that people are professional they must acknowledge the claim of more than the monetary bottom line. Even managers often take more that purely commercial factors into consideratiom in deciding upon policies to pursue. Many professionals utilize highly technical knowledge in doing their work, and some have to judge how much technical knowledge can be legitimately utilized in dealing with persons. So, while there is a conceptual hyphen, which the reader is asked to note at this point, between economics and technology on the one hand, and the professions on the other, there is also a conjunction of concerns. These concerns have appeared on the programs in a number of ways, but this report about them will be limited in scope because the record of the papers and presentations in which they have been discussed is one of the least satisfactory parts of the archives. The discussion of professional and vocational ethics also provides an opportunity to look at some papers dealing with related issues that are not easily placed into the other categories of this study.

1) Biomedical Ethics and Health Care. During the last twenty-five years by far the most prevalent conjunction of professional concerns and ethical reflection has appeared in biomedical ethics. As judged by the amount of literature, the interest aroused, the intensity of involvement, and the extent to which the services of ethicists have been sought out by a professional group to help them think about their work, biomedical ethics has had an unprecedented and unmatched development. If there is a surprise in the history of the Society it is the relatively limited attention paid in its programs to this development. Perhaps members of the Society have been able to discuss the issue in other settings (of which there have been a good many), or have not found the meetings of the Society sufficiently interdisciplinary to make them the best place to deal with these issues.

This is not to say that biomedical ethics have been

overlooked entirely. Papers dealing with various facets of this subject have periodically appeared on the programs since 1965. In that year biomedical ethics was still an embryonic specialty but Joseph Fletcher and Henry Kolbe were paired in a panel on "Ethics and Medicine." Fletcher was an early pioneer in treating the ethical implications of medical practice and spoke largely out of what he had been writing in books like *Morals and Medicine* (Princeton: 1954). In 1974 another panel, with John C. Fletcher, Karen Lebacqz, Richard McCormick, and Paul Ramsey did another general coverage of the subject matter under the title "Current Issues in Bio-medical Ethics." Only John Fletcher's contribution to the panel has surfaced in the research done for this study, and it consisted of an examination of the relationship between abortion decisions following prenatal diagnosis and decisions to forego treatment of newborns with serious handicaps. Fletcher held that there are ethical reasons to support abortion when genetic disorders are involved that do not necessarily hold in cases of active euthanasia with the newborn. In 1978 Joseph Fletcher and L. Harold DeWolf shared a program on "Continuity and Change in Ethics with Special Attention to Medical Technology and Criminal Justice." Fletcher dealt with the medical issues; DeWolf, with the problems of criminal justice, but no papers are available that enable the reconstruction of the session.

Most of the other papers given about biomedical ethics addressed more specific issues. In 1969, for instance, James B. Nelson, Kieran Nolan and Paul Ramsey were members of a panel addressing the topic, "Ethical Methodology and Euthanasia." Ramsey remembers that at the time he was at Georgetown University Medical School preparing his 1969 Beecher lectures and he "soundly speculates" that what he said on that panel is rather like chapter three of the published Beecher Series: *The Patient as Person* (Yale, 1970). The same year Roger L. Shinn gave a paper on "Christian Ethical Methodology and Questions Related to Ethics." Shinn's paper was distributed to members and was followed by the appearance of an article on closely related issues: "Genetic Decisions: A Case Study in Ethical Method," *Soundings* 42 (Fall 1969): 299-310. Shinn suggested that traditional authority and the idea of conforming to nature do not help very much with decisions about genetics, and that utilitarian and pragmatic methods yield only some help. He examined the difficulties of sorting scientific considerations from value judgments, and called genetic manipulation one of the most momentous forms of the human ability to either threaten or enhance human life. In 1976 Karen Lebacqz, David Louisell, Charles McCarthy, and Leroy Walters were together on a panel entitled "Bioethics and Public Policy: The National Commission and the Problem of Fetal Research." In 1980 Daniel E. Lee gave "A Critique of Ramsey's Idea of Quality of Life," and Dennis Doherty, a paper on "the Morality of Non-Punitive Compulsory Sterilization." At the same meeting George Kuykendall looked at the issues that arise in terminal cases in a paper entitled "On Caring for the Dying." This was published with the title "Care for the Dying: A Kübler-Ross Critique," *Theology Today* XXXVIII (April 1981): 37-56.

Three papers given before the Society have focused on the delivery of health care. While each of these papers has raised issues of political policy and economic feasibility, they have never lost track of the conditions that are needed for good medical practice. In 1975 an opening plenary session heard Edward Pelligrino, then of Yale, speak on "Humanizing the Health Care System." Robert L. Shelton has twice considered issues of health care delivery. In 1977 the title of his presentation was "Human Rights and Distributive Justice in Health Care Delivery;" in 1979, "Health Care and Society in China: A Visitor's Report." The first of these papers indicated that interest in this aspect of medical practice--too long neglected--was beginning to become evident in a number of places and that there was a growing consensus that health care is a human right rather than a merely purchasable commodity available to those who can pay for it. This view of the matter is better understood outside of the United States than within our borders. Even so, Shelton observed, even in the United States, which does not formally acknowledge access to health care to be a right, there was (at the time he wrote!) a growing tendency to make it available to all who need it, despite the lack of moral teaching or legal sanction for doing so. But, argued Shelton, this tendency needs a formal financing mechanism that will so order national priorities as to insure it can be implemented. The government is the appropriate instrument for devising such a mechanism. (Little did Shelton foresee that within five or six years a new national administration dedicated to a free market ideology and viewing health care as a commodity would significantly alter the situation and threaten to make the universal delivery of health care highly problematic.) Shelton's 1979 presentation included slides taken on a trip to China. These helped the members of the Society who attended to envision the shape of China's Cultural Revolution and actually to see some of the health care practices associated with it. In commenting on those practices, Shelton took note of the way in which the Chinese are integrating old and traditional medicine with modern means of care, of the wide use of "barefoot doctors" who carry services to the people as para-medics, of the constitutional provision that makes health care a guaranteed right, and of the lack of a Western type national health insurance plan. One of the unique features of the overall program is the emphasis it places on training persons to take responsibility for their own care.

A paper dealing with an issue closely related to health care delivery was included in the 1981 program. James M. Childs, Jr. reported on the "Dialogue with Ross Laboratories: A Chapter in the Infant Formula Controversy." Childs, along with several other church persons, had participated over several months in discussions with Ross Laboratories of Columbus, Ohio (the makers of Similac) as the company sought to determine a responsible stand in the face of the world-wide infant formula debate. The group was received quite openly and was given access to working documents used in drawing up company policy. It was also asked to do some field investigations of the problem. The paper details this experience, indicates the possible dangers of being co-opted, but concludes the church bodies have much to learn and to contribute through this kind of mutual interchange.

One of the most controversial of all medical procedures is the practice of abortion. This issue finds members of the Society deeply divided, not infrequently according to ecclesial identity. The ethical issues stemming from the abortion question arise more from controversy about public policy than from any inherent dilemmas in the medical procedures involved. The Society has discussed the abortion problem only in the last five years. The 1979 John Reeder did a study of "The Relevance of 'Potentiality' in Abortion;" in 1980 Theodore Steeman, a paper on "Ethical Issues in Public Policy Debates on Abortion: A Working Paper;" in 1982, Thomas Shannon, "Abortion and Public Policy: A Review of the Issues;" and in 1983 Marjorie Reiley Maguire, "Covenant, Personhood, and Abortion." Steeman's paper, which has been deposited in the archives in a greatly enlarged and reworked version (with an expression of appreciation for the responses at the time it was given) frankly faced the problems created by different attitudes in different faith traditions, and attempted to bridge the gulf that exists because of them. That gulf was evident, for example, in the controversy over <u>"The Call to Concern,"</u> which was a full page magazine advertisement that many members of the Society signed in 1977 to question the lobbying efforts of the Catholic bishops to cut off federal funds for abortion. <u>"The Call to Concern,"</u> which argued it was unfair to deny poor people access to medical procedures that could be enjoyed by those able to pay for them privately, was a highly controversial matter and much invective as well as appropriate criticism was engendered by it. One of the most valuable meetings in the life of the Society was an unscheduled gathering late one evening at the 1978 meeting at which members of the Society who had participated on both sides of this altercation came together face-to-face and assured each other of mutual respect and a desire to discuss these problems in a continuing way on a scholarly basis.

2) Business Ethics. While the problems related to the practice of medicine have attracted the largest interest, the other professions have also been the subject of scrutiny. The second of all the papers dealing with vocational ethics, which was delivered in 1966 by Robert C. Batchelder, dealt with "Ethics in Business Decision Making: Management Goals and Christian Ethics." Batchelder affirmed the key elements in the management role as a foundation for criticizing certain abuses, and chided those who take a condescending stance toward business. He noted how the goals of management are often complex--seldom merely a simplistic drive to maximize profits--and how the goals of individual managers are frequently even more complex than those of their companies. He then illustrated the kinds of moral choices managers may have to make. Business ethics were not discussed again until 1981, when Donald G. Jones gave a paper, "Ethics and Economics: The Teaching of Business Ethics," which was published in *The Annual*.

3) The Ethics of the Ministry. Ethical problems relating to the role of the clergy were examined in a presidential address given in 1968 by Murray H. Leiffer on "Ethics and Expectations in the Profession of the Ministry." Leiffer was engaged in making an extensive study of attitudes in the clergy in the light of the social changes of the past several decades and had polled a large group of Methodist clergy as one sample and the membership of the Society as another sample. A large percentage in both groups expressed the conviction that organized religion presents a number of problems for those who serve in its professional leadership, though interestingly somewhat fewer members of the Society were critical of church bureaucracies than were those engaged in the pastoral ministry. Both groups were overwhelmingly of the opinion that ministers should be acquainted with the occupational problems of the laity and that the church should be concerned to influence the power structures of society. But, although both samples favored such involvement theoretically, far more members of the Society (95%) expressed a willingness to conduct a civil rights meeting than did the pastors (59%). With regard to the clergyperson's life style, both samples repudiated the idea of a distinctive differentiation of the clergy from the laity, yet, interestingly, the members of the Society were

more inclined than pastors to believe that ministers should live a simple life style regardless of the standards followed by members of their congregations. Leiffer also discovered a decided difference between age groups in attitudes toward participation in civil rights marches and reported many comments on the questionnaires that indicated a major generation gap within the clergy. The problem of participation in social action which Leiffer uncovered has been discussed several times in the life of the Society. It was the subject of James Gustafson's presidential address in 1970 and of a panel in 1975 in which John C. Bennett and Gayraud Wilmore both participated. It was the ongoing focus of concern of the Action/Reflection Interest group.

4) The Ethics of Lawyers. The ethics of lawyers have been the subject of two presentations, both of them made very recently. In 1981 Charles L. Kramer, Jr. gave a paper on Vocations and the Professions: Ethics and Law." This paper, which appears in *The Annual*, focuses attention on both medicine and law, suggesting that the religious concept of vocation furnishes a good basis on which to overcome the tendencies of the professions to neglect the human and social needs of clients. In 1982, Thomas Lombard gave a paper entitled "Ethics and Law: Current Controversy About Professional Ethics of Attorneys." It should be remembered that some of the papers dealing with jurisprudence that were discussed in the previous chapter are germane to the understanding of the lawyer's role in society.

Many years ago, the sociologist Max Weber treated the role and functions of professional groups together. Most of the papers we have reported on in this section have treated just one profession and its ethical problems. Two papers have looked at the professions as a group rather than merely at the problems of a particular group. In 1976 Samuel Calian did a paper on "Toward a Common Ethic Among Professions," which was published in *The Selected Papers* under the title "Ethics and the Professions: Renewal Through Cooperation." Calian scrutinized various professional codes of conduct, including some guidelines for the clergy, and discovered over a dozen similarities. He noted various transitions that were affecting the lives of professionals and examined the prospects for greater interprofessional exchange. In 1981 Karen Lebacqz gave a general treatment of professional ethics under the title "Professional Ethics: Powers and Principalities."

The ethics of pedagogy and governance have been treated in the papers on higher education that are discussed in the next chapter, though it may be a bit of a surprise to see how relatively little attention has been paid to the ethical problems of the teaching profession by a group composed of so many teachers. There has been almost nothing in the program dealing with the problems of those who are engaged in the enforcement of law. Hopefully, we will find ourselves exploring many new dimensions of vocationally related ethics in the years ahead.

10

Other Topics on the Programs

In the previous chapters each of the subject categories discussed was explored in quite a large group of papers. This chapter considers several issues with which a smaller number of papers wrestle, issues that are nevertheless frequently of key importance. It also discusses the attention given in the programs to the teaching of ethics.

Specific Discussions of Jewish, Roman Catholic, and Eastern Orthodox Traditions

Starting as a group with a mainly Protestant orientation, the Society was somewhat slow to pay attention to the contributions of other traditions, even to the traditions which have the same biblical roots as Protestant Christianity. For instance, while the Hebraic heritage of Christian ethics had always been presupposed, it was only the prompting of a special task force, which was formed late in the period being canvassed by this study, that led the Society to give serious attention to the ways in which Jewish ethical thinking has developed alongside the growth of Christian reflection. Likewise, while the common heritage of Protestant and Catholic in the pre-Reformation experience of the church was tacitly assumed, it has only been in the last dozen years that the Society's programs have paid conscious attention to the further development of the Roman Catholic moral tradition as a distinctive entity. Eastern Orthodoxy came to be looked at only in the past few years, when two papers have focused on ethics in that tradition.

1) Jewish Ethics. Ten years after the Society was founded, Charles Kegley gave a paper on "Martin Buber and the Problem of Norms." Kegley identified many Protestant-like elements in the thinking of this Jewish thinker, and suggested that Buber placed a strong emphasis on the relational aspects of ethical decision-making. For Buber, the meaning of the good is integrally related to the will of God, and abstract systems or principles have no place in ethics. But, argued Kegley, Buber's thinking makes a place

for other emphases, such as a Kantian concept of the Absolute--which keeps his ethic from becoming purely situational. According to Kegley, Buber recognized that what are assumed to be divine commands have to be evaluated for legitimacy, and that moral choice cannot be purely arbitrary. Kegley's analysis concluded by noting how Buber's thinking takes due account of the ambiguity involved in ethical decision-making, steering between the Scylla of absolutism and the Charybdis of relativism. After giving his paper before the Society, Kegley published an article entitled "Martin Buber's Ethics and the Problem of Norms," in *Religious Studies* 5, (December 1969): 181-94.

It was six more years before specific attention was again directed to Jewish ethics. In 1975 Sid Z. Leiman gave a paper entitled "The Sinking of the William Brown: A Case Study in Jewish Ethics." This paper examined the moral issues raised by the case of William Brown (whose life boat contained more passengers than it could safely hold). Leiman contrasted the American legal approach to deciding who should be cast overboard, as seen in the adjudication of the case in courts, with how classical Jewish teaching would have approached the same case. Two years later, Robert Willis gave a paper, "Barth, Bonhoeffer, and Jewish Suffering: Reflections on the Relationship Between Theology, Conscience and Moral Action."

In 1979 the task force on Jewish and Christian ethics was becoming active and there was also a growing hope that the membership of the Society might be widened to include a larger number of Jewish scholars. There was a proposal at the time (discussed in the next chapter) to change the name of the Society to The Society of Religious Ethics. In the spirit of that situation Franklin Sherman presented a paper on "Messianism, Mysticism, and the *Mitzvot*: Reflection on the Relation of Jewish and Christian Ethics." His paper, which was chosen for inclusion in *The Selected Papers*, indicated that Jewish ethics can be divided into three types: a "social" type, embodied in messianism; a "dispositional" type embodied in Jewish mysticism; and a "concrete commandment" type as reflected in obedience to the *mitzvot*. The following year Marvin Fox discussed "Contemporary Trends in Jewish Ethics," and his paper was also published in *The Selected Papers*. In its published form, Fox's paper was entitled "Reflections on the Foundations of Jewish Ethics and Their Relation to Public Policy." It notes that much philosophical work remains to be done in articulating Jewish ethics, and shows--by suggesting how various Jewish teachers have dealt in quite divergent ways with particular problems--how much variation is encountered in Jewish thinking. According to Fox, Jewish scholars differ on theoretical questions such as the cognitive foundation of ethics, the proper justification of norms and the relationship of law and morality. Jewish ethicists also come to different positions on questions of public policy, even though they generally teach that government should be just and that the state must not override the commandment of God. Hence, they work under the same limitations as Christian ethicists, and their witness as spokespersons for their tradition is affected by the same problems as face Christian ethicists.

In 1981, Ronald Green's paper, "The Korah Episode: A Rationalist Reappraisal of Rabbinic Anti-Rationalism," which was published in *The Annual*, examined the problem of revelation and reason as found in Jewish ethics. Noting the argument as to whether or not Jewish ethics support the idea of rational autonomy in the moral life, Green cited Midrashic and Talmudic commentary on the argument over the authority of Moses found in the Korah episode in Numbers 16. Holding that the crucial issue is not whether a given religious tradition openly acknowledges the supremacy of reason, but "whether its own revealed sources of authority do or do not invariably support rationally defensible moral conduct," Green concluded that the Jewish treatment of the Korah incident suggests that a rapprochement is possible between a religious tradition that relies on revelation for its authority and a rationalism that looks at the basic fabric of a religious heritage in order to sense the role of reasoning in the complex and sophisticated dimensions of its beliefs.

In 1980 Sumner B. Twiss and David A. Wiener gave a paper on "Moral Responsibility in Mishnah," and Wayne G. Boulton, a paper on "Jewish Christian Ethics in the 80's: A Constructive Statement." Boulton's paper was addressed to Christians on the American right wing, calling them to acknowledge their indebtedness to Judaism more candidly and to accept social responsibility within the larger family of communities whose life is patterned on law. Presenting a model of Jewish Christian ethics inspired by the ethos of the Hillel order of the Pharisees, Boulton showed how this model was affected by the concept of covenant as a vertical dimension and by "constitutionalism" as a horizontal dimension. Its breadth provided an effective means of counteracting anti-Judaism both inside and outside of the Christian community.

Two papers dealing with the holocaust may be mentioned in connection with Jewish ethics even though they focus more on a Jewish related question than on the specific nature of Jewish ethics as such. One of these was given in 1981 by John T. Pawlikowski and was entitled "The Holocaust: Its Implications for Public Morality." The other, in 1983, by

Hans O. Teifel, was on "Rethinking Christian Ethics in Light of the Holocaust." Both of these papers are in the archives. Pawlikowski authored an article, "The Holocaust: Its Implications for the Church and Society Problematic," *Encounter* 42, (Spring 1981): 143-54. Both writers were equally disturbed by the Holocaust and anxious to avoid any repetition of its horror. But they had somewhat different explanations for why it took place. Pawlikowski argued that the holocaust was related to the rise of aggressive secularism which eclipsed the dimension of transcendence from public consciousness. He suggested the importance of recapturing a religious criticism over the human enterprise. Tiefel charged that the churches were silent partners or tacit accomplices in the horror and were unwilling to speak in defense of the Jews. Back of this unwillingness, argued Tiefel, was a tacit theological anti-Semitism. The culture also contributed to the problem because it set the stage for a detached professionalism which isolated certain kinds of human activity from moral scrutiny. Both of these causes, he suggested, arose out of a culture shaped by the dualistic social ethic of German Protestantism. Using this diagnosis, Tiefel called for a strategy that places public life under the continual scrutiny of religious faith and that recognizes the common Lordship of God over both Israel and the church.

2) Roman Catholic Moral Theology. The discussion of the Roman Catholic heritage as a specific tradition began at the 1972 meeting. At that meeting Warren Reich gave a paper on "The Unity of Personal and Social Ethics in the Theology of Karl Rahner," (which cannot be located). Charles Curran, in a presidential address, examined "Catholic Ethics Today in Light of the Dialogue with Protestant Ethics." In his address Curran examined post-Vatican II changes in Roman Catholic moral theology taking place as a result of the emerging dialogue between Catholics and Protestants. He took issue with the distinctions drawn between the thinking of the two groups developed in Roger Mehl's book *Catholic Ethics and Protestant Ethics*, arguing that Mehl over emphasized the differences between the two traditions. According to Curran, Roman Catholic moral theology had been engaged in a far more thorough critique of its own natural law heritage than Mehl had indicated--a critique that brought it closer to Protestant ways of doing ethics than commonly realized, and which provided it with a plurality of methodologies to replace the codified tradition in the moral theology handbooks of the triumphalist period.

According to Curran, the role of the teaching authority of the Church had been undergoing reconceptualization. For instance, many moral theologians were arguing that on certain matters papal authority could be considered provisional rather than infallible. This development was resulting in an increasing pluralism in the Church. Finally, changes in theological presuppositions of Catholic thinking were modifying the nature/supernature issue and making the Church's position nearer to one of Christ transforming culture than of Christ above culture. Roman Catholic thinking was also shifting, argued Curran, in ways that made it impossible to stress sanctification to the exclusion of justification, or order at the expense of freedom. Curran noted that Protestant ethicists, the Roman Catholic community in general, and even the bishops and members of the hierarchical teaching office of the Roman church herself had often been unaware of these changes in the thinking of moral theologians.

In 1976, James M. Gustafson gave a paper entitled "Overcoming Differences in Catholic and Protestant Ethics." This paper shared with the Society work in progress toward the publication of his book *Protestant and Roman Catholic Ethics* (University of Chicago Press, 1978).

3) Eastern Orthodoxy. This was the last specific tradition to be discussed. In 1977 Stanley Harakas delivered a paper, "Natural Law in Christian Ethics: An Eastern Orthodox Perspective." This was published, under a slightly modified title, in *The Selected Papers*. Harakas has further developed his materials and published a book, *Toward Transfigured Life: The Theoria of Eastern Orthodox Ethics* (Light and Life Publishing Company, 1983). In the paper before the Society, Harakas pointed out that Eastern Orthodox thinking has always made a place for natural law, but has given it only casual attention. In natural law thinking in the Eastern tradition, equity is an important consideration--a fact that gives natural law in that tradition an important social import. The natural law is connected with the teaching of the Decalogue--although the Decalogue is seen as but a limited aspect of Christian morality. The commandments are important, but are understood in connection with a larger sense of God's being, will, and purpose.

A paper by Vigen Guorian in 1983, "Notes Toward an Eastern Orthodox Ethics," pointed out that Eastern theology moves in an experiential and practical way from a discussion of virtue to reflection on the nature of love, and from reflection on love to the exploration of mystical union with God. Eastern Orthodoxy has not accorded ethics the independence from theology it tends to have in Protestantism, nor has it been rigorously systematic in its approach. Nevertheless, it has stressed *theosis* (conforming to the nature of God) and love as cardinal concepts. It sees the Incarnation as making something close to the imitation of Christ important for the Christian life--but does so without the Pelagian rationalism that is often associated with the concept of imitation of Christ in Western understandings. Eastern thinking disagrees with all utilitarian, deontological, or teleological ethics which treat the world with either a utilitarian or rational calculus. For Eastern thought the goal of ethics is to achieve salvation as oneness with God.

Excursion into Comparative Religious Ethics

Just as the Society broadened its scope of inquiry to include Jewish, Roman Catholic, and Eastern Orthodox traditions, so to a lesser extent it has examined ethical reflection in other faith traditions. Five papers and one panel in programs of the Society have examined ethics in the non-Western world.

In 1966 two papers were focused on such concerns. "Pushing Back the Inscrutable: Research in Religion and Social Change in Hindu and Buddhist Ethics" was the title of a presentation by Bardwell Smith. He was working on these issues at the time and some months later published an article, "Toward a Buddhist Anthropology: The Problem of the Secular," in *The Journal of the American Academy of Religion* 36, (September 1968): 203-16. Robert E. Lee's paper "Stranger in the Land: Ethical Speculation in Japan," given the same year, was later used as the basis of an article "Obstacles to Church Growth," in *Theology Today* 32, (April 1966): 73-87.

Five years later, a major plenary session was devoted to "Ethics in the Non-Western World." Rubem Alves, then teaching at Union Seminary in New York but speaking from a South American orientation, discussed the "Crisis of Imagination in Western Ethics." J. DeOtis Roberts of Howard University explored "African Religions and African Social Consciousness." Hideo Hashimoto of Lewis and Clark College examined the "Renewal of Buddhism in Japan: Moral and Political Significance." Hashimoto's paper survives in a blue dittoed form in the archives in a version more extensive than could have been presented on the program. The paper examines the feelings of destitution, emptiness, despair and defeat in Japan following the end of the Second World War, and looks at the conditions that gave rise to new religious groups, particularly the movement known as Nicheren Shoshu Sokagakkai. Many of the observations made by Hashimoto resemble the kind of analysis a sociologist would make of a new sect, but he did include observations about the basic ethical stance of the new group. Hashimoto saw the movement as a kind of "situation ethics" carried to the extreme. He noted how the movement embraced contradictory elements even without holding them in dialectical tension. The will of the leader, whatever form it takes, is decisive. The organization expects unquestioning obedience and in return provides a strong sense of belonging. The movement, in emphasizing the importance of work, has features similar to the Protestant ethic, but has nothing akin to the Protestant principle, which enables a group to criticize its own life from within. It has no sense of guilt, sin, or grace.

It was another five years before the program of the Society again contained a presentation on non-Christian traditions. In 1976 Roderick Hindery presented "Ethics in Hinduism, Buddhism, and Confucianism: Some Methodological Questions." Hindery had given considerable attention to these matters and the same year in which he delivered this paper before the Society he published "Hindu Ethics in the Ramayana" in *The Journal of Religious Ethics* 4 (Fall 1976): 287-322. In 1982 George L. Frear contributed to cross-cultural understandings with a paper entitled "The Iroquois Experience of Good and Evil." Frear outlined the creation stories of the Iroquois tribe, in which twin deities function, and he examined the dualistic assumptions in the tribe's healing practices. He showed how later changes in Iroquois ritual modified the dualism of the creation myth, but commended Iroquois thinking generally for taking very seriously the possibility that evil is, to use a phrase from Paul Ricouer, "an original element of being." The last paper dealing with ethics in another religious tradition was delivered in 1983, when Frederick S. Carney examined "Obligation and Virtue in Islamic and Western Ethics."

Ethics and Liturgy

In the first section of this history we indicated that there was much vacillating in program planning about the inclusion of worship as part of the regularly scheduled activities of the annual meeting. Whatever the ambivalence about holding services of worship, there has been no question about having occasional sessions of the program deal with the relationship between ethics and liturgy. There have been a number of such discussions, but they did not begin to appear on the program of the Society until well into the second decade of its life.

In 1972 a panel consisting of Richard Davis, Paul Elman, and William Everett discussed the relationship between "The Cultic and the Political." Everett's contribution to the panel was published in *The Anglican Theological Review* 56 (January 1974): 16-34, under the title, "Liturgy and American Society: An Invocation for Ethical Analysis." With bold and broad strokes Everett examined the role played by liturgy in civic religion, in the sports programs of universities, and in movements for wide-spread cultural and social change. Everett found a key relationship to exist between ritual and the legitimation of authority, and noted that the presence of liturgical kinds of behavior in so many areas of public life had consequences for the churches. Roman Catholics, in whose tradition liturgical reform started in the late nineteenth century as an effort to recover the sources of liturgical practice, have moved increasingly to celebrations related to issues of peace and justice. Protestants, whose worship has often been an expression of the thrust toward self-control over the decisions of life, have frequently discovered liturgical meaning in the struggle for social justice. In the future, suggested Everett, there will be even more interchange between the worship of the churches and their social environment. Both students of ethics and students of liturgy must become more aware of the various patterns in which people exercise their social roles--patterns having both liturgical and ethical meaning.

At the 1978 meeting Paul M. Harrison gave a paper with the title: "Dramaturgy and Ethics." Harrison had just published an essay entitled "Toward a Dramaturgical Interpretation of Religion," *Sociological Analysis* 38 (Winter 1977): 389-396, which drew attention to theatricality and dramaturgy as modes of interpreting religious behavior. While his paper as delivered before the Society is not available, Harrison shared with this writer a mimeographed article from which he developed from it, entitled "A Dramaturgical Interpretation of Theological Ethics." Harrison's paper raised issues on the boundary line between ethics and liturgics. According to Harrison, the dramaturgist looks carefully at a process in which virtues and habits are developed in shared interactional situations, and thus has insights that may contribute to a profounder understanding of ethics--particularly of those ways of doing ethics that emphasize the role of story, the place of character, and the importance of interactional relationships in the making of decisions. Admittedly, Harrison was less directly concerned for liturgy in the specific sense of religious worship or civic ceremony than Everett, but his paper did indicate how the dramas of public life interrelate to social values and the appeal which those values have to the public. He concluded that the doing of ethics cannot be merely a dispassionate, non-theatrical, publicly rational exercise, but must see how people are involved in moral dramas. All modes of drama have implications for morality and ethics, not merely (as many ethicists have supposed) the mode of tragedy.

Considerable attention was given to the relationship

between ethics and liturgy at the 1979 meeting, when a plenary session was devoted to a discussion of this topic. Paul Ramsey was asked to address the subject on a panel with Donald Saliers, who teaches worship at the Candler School of Theology in Atlanta. Margaret Farley responded. All three parts of this session were published in the Fall 1979 issue of *The Journal of Religious Ethics*, along with additional responses later prepared by William Everett and Philip J. Rossi. In his presentation, Ramsey examined how both liturgy and morality refer to the divine events to which faith also testifies and argued that an ethicist's understanding of morality is diminished without a grasp of the content of liturgy and the rule of faith. Examining the role of liturgy in relation to the practice of marriage, Ramsey explored with some care the practice of Eastern Orthodox churches in using a special (and different) liturgy for the marriage of divorced persons than it uses for the first marriage of partners. The ritual for a marriage of divorced parties contains an explicit acknowledgement of shortcoming and failure--an emphasis that Ramsey finds salutary in its witness to the essential indissolubility of the marriage bond. Contrasting the realism of the Eastern Orthodox ritual with the sentimentality of a liturgy remembered from the days of his participation in Youth Fellowship, Ramsey made some telling points about his belief in the importance of structure and fidelity in marriage.

In his presentation, Donald Saliers focused on the role of liturgy in the formation of the moral agent. He stressed the corporate nature of worship as an experience which shapes character. He looked at four modalities of corporate prayer--thanksgiving, anamnesis, confession and intercession--and the role which is played by each in Christian development. While explicitly repudiating any reduction of worship to a merely instrumental significance in shaping the moral agent, Saliers showed how the worship of God can call forth obedience to the Gospel and maintain prophetic self-awareness in a world of moral ambiguity. Saliers urged ethicists to pay more attention to the role of liturgy in the shaping of those communities in which decisions are made and carried out. He also urged liturgists to be more astute in considering how their efforts can nurture the affections and virtues requisite for the moral life.

Margaret Farley emphasized that the failure and impoverishment of contemporary worship may well stem from the ethical shortcomings in the church--injustice in its life, disagreement as to the importance and the nature of the service that should be rendered to the world, and a breakdown of the symbols which point to inclusion and justice for all. She suggested that worship will become rich and meaningful only as the ethical roots of community are reconstructed.

In 1983 Richard Bondi considered "Christian Ethics and the Formation of Character: The Role of the Sermon." Setting his discussion in an overview of the ethics of character and virtue, and noting the importance of hearing the story as a factor in the formation of character, Bondi examined where and how the Christian story is told. He identified six places: scripture; church history; ritual; preaching; the transmission and editing of Christian thought; and the lives and witness of present-day Christians. The sermon, which most directly implements the fourth of these ways, renders the images, symbols, and implications of the story available to the hearts of a particular congregation. Drawing on the several principles of narrative preaching set forth in the work of Professor F. B. Craddock, he examined the promise and danger in a narrative style of preaching and indicated ways in which the ethicist can serve a useful function by acting as editor (and not merely as recounter) of the story.

Papers and Programs Dealing with the Ethics of Sex

In the first twenty-five years of the Society's history the ethics of sexual behavior have been dealt with eleven times on the programs of the annual meetings. All of these occasions have occurred in the last fifteen years. The archives do not have a very complete record of the various presentations, but some trends can be traced from what is available.

In 1968 Paul Ramsey moderated a plenary session on "Changing Sex Ethics and Value Patterns in the Modern World." Bernard Häring, serving at the time as a Visiting Professor at Union Theological Seminary, gave the paper and George Easter responded. Häring's paper is not available. Easter's response--which is a substantive discussion in its own right--explored a situational understanding of sexual morality. Referring to Häring's book, *The Law of Christ*, Easter noted how Häring moves directly from a discussion of responsibility to an exposition of normative patterns. Easter questioned whether such a move is licit, and argued that a strong situationalism (in which future behavior is not necessarily guided by past experience) would provide a more satisfactory approach, since openness to the new and to the unexpected constitute an important aspect of sexual fulfillment.

Seven years later, in 1975, Margaret Farley presented a paper on "Sexuality and Sexual Identity," with John H. McNeill and Robert Beene responding. The next year John Giles Milhaven's topic was, "Christian Evaluations of Sexual Pleasure." His paper is found in *The Selected Papers* 1976.

Milhaven's paper reflected materials earlier documentated and explained in an article in *Theological Studies* 35 (December, 1974: 692-710. He outlined four different evaluations of sexual pleasure given in Christian thought. In one of these, the pleasure is acknowledged to be good but is deemed as something that should be sought only in conjunction with the desire to procreate; in another the desire for pleasure is considered an essential aspect of the relationship and is to be sought for its value in enhancing the conjugal relationship; in a third the pleasure is accepted as legitimate but not considered the essential quality of the relation between partners; and in the fourth the pleasure is considered foul and evil. Even though the fourth position looks at sexual pleasure as something that needs to be forgiven and should never be sought as an end in itself, it treats sex as something that may be used by God in the furtherance of His purposes in creating new souls. Several months after delivering his paper before the Society, Milhaven published "Thomas Aquinas on Sexual Pleasure," *The Journal of Religious Ethics* 5 (Fall, 1977): 7-58.

In 1977 Beverly Harrison, joined with her husband, James Harrison, in preparing a paper entitled "Normative Problems in Family Ethics," which was published in *The Selected Papers* under the title "Some Problems for Normative Christian Family Ethics." In this paper, delivered by Beverly Harrison, certain reservations are expressed about traditional Christian teaching about marriage. The paper emphasizes a belief that marriage should be thought of as a relational life process more than as a particular status bestowed by civil or religious authority, and that the quality of interpersonal relations rather than the existence of a particular institutionalized status should be of primary concern. Charging that marriage as an institution is "being asked to bear the burden of compensation for depersonalizing, alienating life elsewhere in society," the paper contends that there is a pervasive need to cultivate capacities of intimacy that are free of manipulation and coercion.

"The Duty to Desire: Love, Friendship, and Sexuality in Some Puritan Theories of Marriage," is the title of a paper given by Edmund Leites at the 1980 meeting. This paper was published in *The Comparative Civilization Review* (Fall 1979): 40-82. In this paper Leites shows that the Puritan notion of conjugal love was one which held that "an outward fulfillment of the duties of marriage was not enough; the proper intention and feelings toward your spouse also had to exist." Leites's paper suggests that the Puritans did sense the importance of some of the very qualities the Harrisons were upholding, and it also hints at some of the reasons the Puritan ethos was not as successful as it could have been in providing spouses with the means to attain the qualities of interaction which it held up as the ideal.

At the 1981 meeting, Wilson Yates gave a paper on "the Family and Power: Towards an Ethic of Family Social Responsibility." This paper appears in *The 1981 Annual*. Yates focused attention on the family as a unit of power in society, and urged Christian ethicists to consider the social responsibilities incumbent on families in the exercise of their power. Perhaps this paper should be mentioned under another rubric---such as political ethics--since it was much concerned with how the family functions as a unit of social influence in the political and economic order. It had relatively little to say abut sexual morality in the usual sense of that term, but it does prompt us to wonder how participation in external power configurations affects intimate relationships. Another paper at the 1981 meetings, by Roger B. Betsworth, given at the meeting under the title "Sexual Values, 1980," and found in the archives under the title "Sexual Responsibility: An Analysis of Mutuality," examines the ideal of mutuality found in the writings of Masters and Johnson and argues that the ideal cannot sustain itself in contemporary culture. Betsworth argued that only as a couple copes with experiences of betrayal and goes beyond competitive manipulation will it be able to sustain the marriage relationship. This involves reversing the ordinary logic of equivalency and reciprocal mutuality and finding a grace that heals experiences of suffering and tragedy.

In 1982 Carl A. Raschke gave a paper on "Homosexuality and the Construction of Christian Ethics." The same year, James E. Allen of the School of Public Health, gave a paper on "Women's Challenge to Christian Ethics: Notions of the Family." The subtitle of Allen's paper was "Why the Women's Movement Challenges Basic Assumptions in Western Christian Ethics about the Functions of the Family, Reproduction, and Work."

Two sessions dealing with sexual morality were on the program of the twenty-fourth annual meeting in 1983. David F. Kelley gave a paper on "Sexuality and Concupiscence in Augustine." Drawing together certain texts of Augustine and analyzing Augustine's teaching about sex in the context of those passages, this paper argues that while Augustine explicitly intended to teach for human kind, to help his readers and hearers live more fully, and to further the beauty of Christian married life, his understanding of the act of sexual pleasure and desire in carnal concupiscence did not achieve that result because it tainted human sexuality with implications of evil and corruption. This paper was published in *The Annual*. The second session dealing with this topic at the 1983 meeting was a panel on the teaching of sexual ethics. This panel was chaired by James B. Nelson, and Robert W. Blaney, Christine Gudorf, John Giles Milhaven, and Jane Cary Peck were participants.

Higher Education

The great majority of the members of the Society are involved in some form of higher education. Yet, in only five papers, concentrated in two programs of the Society, has attention been directed to higher education and the ethical issues that arise in either pedagogy or governance. Perhaps higher education is relatively free of moral problems; perhaps it is easier to speculate how to resolve the problems of others than to resolve our own; perhaps it cuts too close to the tender quick when directing attention to things so near home.

The 1968 meeting had three papers dealing with problems of higher education. This was the time of campus ferment and that may explain the sudden and isolated concentration of attention to this subject at that meeting. Two of these papers were part of a panel entitled "Power and Dissent in Educational Institutions." Louis Joughlin of the American Association of University Professors spoke on "Institutional Identities and Purposes," and Samuel H. Magill, on "Academic Freedom and Participation." Magill argued that academic freedom involves three dimensions: 1) the right of the teacher-scholar to pursue truth wherever it might lead and to profess understandings of that truth according to the best possible judgment that can be mustered; 2) the right of students (and faculty) to hear speakers from a wide spectrum of viewpoints and to enjoy "due process" in how they are treated under institutional policies; and 3) the right of a community of scholars to articulate its own goals and to define its own norms and priorities. Magill contrasted the "law of the jungle"--which governs where redress of grievances is not possible through rational and legal means--with the ideal of the university as a place which upholds a principle of adjudicating claims on the basis of merit. He asked how much politics by confrontation constitute a threat to the university's *raison de être*. He looked at hierarchical, negotiational, and participatory models of governance, and examined the reasons why the participatory model has not worked as effectively in practice as ideally might be expected. He concluded that only when all of the constituencies of the university share a commitment to some common center of values, know how to communicate with each other about those shared values, and are required to exercise power under restraints that make them responsible to all the other constituencies in appropriate ways, will institutional governance have the quality it ought to have.

At the same meeting Robert E. Fitch overviewed "Changing Student Roles and Expectations." He found five different attitudinal groups with which it is possible to identify, and listed five "gaps" that exist between those groups on the campus. He set up a spectrum with "hippies," at one end and "hoodlums" at the other. He criticized the "hippies" as largely hypocritical and the "hoodlums" as threats to the civility of the university. He suggested the central majority of the student citizens of the academic world are quite uninterested in being involved in either of these extremes.

In 1975, the only other annual meeting to consider ethical issues of higher education, C. Freeman Sleeper gave a paper on "College as a Moral Community." He identified the areas of moral concern on campus, examined the broader social trends which impinge on college life, and noted how moral choices are forced on the college by both external influences and internal pressures. According to Sleeper, colleges will only be able to handle the moral issues confronting them as they define what it means to be a moral community. The other paper in 1975 was given by Edward L. Long, Jr. on "Credibility in Campus Governance." Long argued that educational institutions must govern themselves according to some agreed upon goals and purposes and that they must rely almost completely on persuasion in the making of decisions. They cannot rely upon the exercise of power as the main instrument of governance. To embrace power as a means of deciding issues invites those with more power who wish to interfere with the university's affairs to ignore the openness which the university cherishes. None of the papers discussed in this section has ever been published.

Papers and Programs Dealing with the Teaching of Ethics and the Role of Ethicists in Academia and the Church

One of the original reasons for bringing together teachers of Christian ethics was to exchange ideas about teaching the field and to talk together about professional responsibilities in school, in church, and in society. The presidential address of Das Kelley Barnett at the constituting meeting of the Society in 1959 was devoted largely to trying to define the nature of Christian ethics as a discipline. It also pointed to the need to exchange ideas about teaching and the professional roles of the Christian ethicist. (Copies of that address have not been found in the research done for this history, but there have been several recollections of it made by those who were present at the founding meeting.)

A long series of papers, panels, and workshops dealing with these matters has taken place in subsequent years. In all but nine of the twenty-five years of the Society's history there has been at least one, and in one year as many as three, parts of the program devoted to the discussion of how to teach the field. In the second year of the Society's history, almost the entire program was devoted to a discussion of pedagogical aspects of the profession. Indeed, the only other item on the agenda of that meeting was an address by Reinhold Niebuhr. In the next year, 1961, a session on the case method in the teaching of Christian ethics was planned, though it seems to have been cancelled because the scheduled speaker was unable to get there. (See chapter one for additional details on these two meetings).

The presidential address of E. Clinton Gardner in 1962 was on "The Church and Its Social Witness." Gardner applied the typology in H. Richard Niebuhr's *Christ and Culture* to the relationship of the church to society. He proposed a model for the contemporary witness of the church that incorporates elements of both the dualist and the transformationist types. He took the transformation of society as the goal of the church, but noted that since this transformation is never complete, the strategy of the church must include maintaining the eschatological tension between the Gospel and the culture. The following year, Kenneth Smith delivered a paper on "The Churches and the Sociology of the Future."

There are two other papers in the archives of the 1963 meeting that deal with matters germane to this rubric. Thomas Oden reported on his experiment with the use of research and dialogue teams in teaching. He noted the sociological context of his teaching--a context dominated by a cultural Protestantism which either prompted withdrawal from the realm of political affairs or sanctioned the absorption of the culture's values by the church. To counteract the mind-set of such culture-Protestantism, Oden set up teams of students who undertook to dialogue, not only with each other about the reading assignments, but with the local community about its problems and conditions. His paper reported on the results of the experiment, utilizing information gathered from questionnaires returned by class members at the conclusion of the course. This paper provides a detailed account of an unusual way of teaching. In the program for the same year, George D. Younger examined an action/research project on juvenile delinquency conducted on the lower East side of Manhattan. In addition to reporting on what was actually done, Younger examined several theoretical issues being addressed in social work circles and the possible connection between those issues and the problems that ought to be raised by the Christian social ethicist.

In 1966, under the leadership of Joseph Fletcher, and again in 1969, under the leadership of Henry B. Clark and

Donald W. Shriver, Jr., attention was directed at the use of the case method for the teaching of Christian social ethics. Fletcher's presentation reflected the then popular status of the situation ethics approach. Clark had conducted a survey among members of the Society concerning their teaching methods and gave a written report based on replies from some twenty-six members of the Society, twenty of whom used the case method in teaching. Some of those who replied indicated that they used the case method for entire courses; others interspersed case method teaching with other techniques. A catalog of the values and dangers in using the method was included in Clark's report. Donald Shriver compiled a four-page list of pertinent resources, including theoretical discussion of cases, analytical treatments of the method's value, instruction in the use of the method, game theory, and a list of individuals using these techniques and willing to be contacted for further information about them.

The case method for teaching social ethics is as old as the discipline, having been used by Francis Greenwood Peabody in the 1880s in his course at Harvard which initiated the discipline in America. But the lure of the case method in the Society's life was possibly felt most strongly in the heyday of situationalism. In 1974 there was yet another panel on "The Use of the Case-Study Approach," in which Keith Bridston, Frederick Carney, George Crowell, Donald Shriver, and J. Philip Wogaman participated. The panel was scheduled right after the annual banquet (which at that point in the Society's history was a relatively unused hour) and consisted of informal sharing between panel members and the audience about their experiences with this way of teaching. The case study method had also figured prominently in the paper delivered by Keith Bridston in 1974 discussed in chapter nine.

Meanwhile, other aspects of the teaching of ethics were considered in program presentations. In 1970 there was a panel entitled "Training Agents for Social Change." Sister Martin de Fores Gray and Albert Sampson made presentations which have not be found. The presentation by a third panelist, George Crowell, is available. It focused particularly on ways in which we can train students to work actively to eliminate evils such as racism from the social order. Crowell expressed his concern that the theoretical instruction we usually provide does little to prepare students to undertake social action, and described an interdisciplinary program for teaching the skills of social action being instituted at the University of Windsor. While the program was designed to concentrate on the study of social action, thus preparing people for more active roles in their communities, it would not require students to participate in any particular cause. Over a decade later, in 1981, George Younger gave a paper, "Action Training: A Contribution to the Church's Witness in Modern Society," which reported on some experiments he was conducting at the time.

In 1973 a workshop of the teaching of ethics was arranged by Frederick Carney. Four members of the Society--Joseph L. Allen, Charles C. West, Charles Reynolds, and Daniel C. Maguire--participated. Each of them answered these two questions: "What am I doing in the teaching of ethics?" and "How do I think this can best be achieved?" The responses were mimeographed and distributed to members of the Society, and are in that form in the archives. The persons on this panel were teaching in quite different schools and even in quite different contexts, so there was some breadth to the answers which they gave. Even so, some of the problems they encountered in their work seem to be common to all the settings in which they worked. Maguire's presentation included a kind of pie chart of the type that would soon thereafter appear in his book *The Moral Choice* (Doubleday, 1978).

Game theory, rather than the case method, provided the framework of two other programs dealing with the teaching of ethics. In 1975 Thomas R. McFall, Robert Mansbach, Harry L. Smith, and Robert W. Terry led a workshop called, "Teaching through Simulation Games." In 1977 Ronald Green gave a paper on "A Game for the Teaching of Ethics." As yet unpublished, Green's paper describes the use of the game for demonstrating to a class of students the difficulties of making choices in social situations.

There have also been sessions devoted to the problems of teaching about specific issues. In 1977 Darell Reeck gave a paper on "Teaching Ethics on Global Issues." His paper included an analysis of *Limits of Growth* by Meadows and Meadows, and showed how, by using contrasting models, the place of assumption as well as the significance of empirical elements in a decision could be demonstrated. Mention has already been made of the panel on the teaching of sexual ethics that was held in 1983.

Along with the papers dealing with the teaching of Christian ethics, other papers have considered the professional vocation of the Christian ethicist outside of the purely academic role. In 1977, Dieter T. Hessel looked at "Solidarity Ethics: A Public Focus for the Church." In his paper Hessel criticized both the churches and the Christian ethicists for their failure to be more concerned with urgent policy questions and concrete forms of the struggle for social justice. He suggested that taking the idea of solidarity between peoples as a central key for the doing of ethics would help ethics to relate to where the law is lived, where justice is done, where love is expressed, and where community is reinforced. This is one of the few papers given before the Society over the years dealing with pedagogical issues or professional concerns that has been published. It appears in *The Selected Papers 1977*.

Certain other papers have been directed to even broader aspects of the professional role of the Christian ethicist. Two other presentations, both given in 1979, deserve mention. Karen Lebacqz, Carl Marbury, and Howard Hills discussed "Professional Ethicists in Non-academic Roles" at that meeting. Edward L. Long, Jr., in a special afternoon session, helped to celebrate the twentieth anniversary of the Society with a preliminary account of its history, and at that time made a promise to prepare a longer version in connection with the twenty-fifth anniversary.

This concludes the account of the programs of the Society--programs that have examined an enormous range of issues in a great variety of ways to the edification of a large proportion of those who are actively engaged in the teaching of Christian ethics in the United States and Canada. The last section of this history will reflect on the significance of the Society's achievements and on its prospects for the future.

Part Four
Analysis

11

Toward the Scholarly Nurture of a Prophetic Witness

This volume is a study of the conception, growth, and coming to age of a professional organization. If the Society were a human being we could tell much about it at the twenty-fifth anniversary of its birth. A person at twenty-five years of age has undergone more physical development than that person is likely to undergo in the remainder of life. While still "young," that person has acquired full physical growth (except for accretions of fat), basic motor skills, most of the capacity for cognitive learning, and much of the knowledge needed to thrive in the natural and social worlds. The main personality traits are identifiable, if not the maturity and wisdom that come later. Moreover, a person at twenty-five has probably become located in the role, or roles, that will be played out in greater complexity and detail during the remaining years of life.

It would be hazardous to suggest that an organization at its twenty-fifth year stands in an exactly analogous position. The comparison between individuals and groups dare not be pushed very far--though neither does the comparison need to be repudiated altogether. It is legitimate to ask whether the Society of Christian Ethics has now approached a kind of maximized growth, whether the present programs of the Society adequately deal with the range of Christian ethics as a discipline, whether or not the Society has already discovered the skills and procedures that will mark its life for an indefinite future, and what it would mean for a young Society such as this to pass into mature adulthood.

The Society and the Field

The disciplinary focus of the Society has been called both Christian ethics and by the closely related term Christian social ethics. In fact, as we will see in the discussion below, the Society first designated itself with the second of these terms and then moved to the first.

As fields of learning, both of these terms delineate intellectual pursuits that are far older than the Society. Hence it is important not to equate the history of the Society with the history of an academic discipline. Christian ethics is as old as Christianity itself and even has roots in Old Testament thought. It pays attention to philosophical ethics, which go back to the pre-Socratics, if not to earlier figures. A history of Christian ethics resembles a history of Christian thought and is integrally related to it. Moral theology, which is mainly a Roman Catholic designation, has been taught as preparation of confessors for many centuries. Protestants also use the term theological ethics, which is contrasted with philosophical ethics and is as old as moral reasoning about the good life.

Christian social ethics as a consciously defined field, on the other hand, can be said to have a shorter history. To be sure the Christian churches have always had social teaching, as Ernst Troeltsch has made us aware in his famous history. But teaching about social problems in a way that would translate ethics into action, which is probably the main focus of Christian social ethics, stands at the centennial of its history rather than at the conclusion of its first twenty-five years. James Dombrowski has recounted the origins of such teaching in his book *The Early Days of Christian Socialism in America* (Columbia University Press, 1936). Dombrowski reports on the surging growth of instruction in social issues at universities and seminaries during the 1880's and 1890's. Such instruction was frequently called by the term Christian sociology or ecclesiastical sociology when offered in schools of divinity, and not infrequently was concerned with social problems in a way that would be somewhat similar to what is now taught by many members of the Society. The academic year 1883-84, which stands just a hundred years prior to the twenty-fifth anniversary which occasions this volume, can be taken as a touchstone for the beginning of Christian social ethics as a special academic undertaking. That is the date which several historians give to the first regularly presented American university course in social ethics as taught in Harvard's curriculum by Francis Greenwood Peabody. (Barton J. Bernstein, "Francis Greenwood Peabody: Conservative Social Reformer," *New England Quarterly* 36, [September, 1963]: 320-337; Jurgen Herbst, "Francis Greenwood Peabody: Harvard's Theologian of the Social Gospel," *Harvard Theological Review* 54, [January 1961]: 55; and Samuel Eliot Morison, *Three Centuries of Harvard: 1636-1936* [Harvard University Press, 1946]: 377.)

Peabody taught social ethics to students of both the

College and the Divinity School. Of the reasons leading him to teach that course Professor Peabody wrote:

> I was led to my subject by a somewhat different road from most of those who deal with it. As a teacher of ethics I became aware of the chasm which exists between such abstract study and the practical applications of moral ideals; and it seemed to me possible to approach the theory of ethics inductively, through the analysis of social movements, which could be easily characterized and from which principles could be deduced. I studied thus with my class the problems of Charity, Divorce, the Indians, the Labor Problem, Intemperance, with results of surprising interest. . . the students felt a living interest in the subjects treated; and I think they will be more publicly spirited as citizens and more discreet as reformers by even this slight opportunity for research [offered in this class]. There is in this department a new opportunity in university instruction. With us it has been quite without precedent. It summons young men who have been imbued with the principles of political economy and of philosophy to the practical application of those studies. It ought to do what college work rarely does--bring a young man's studies near to the problems of an American's life. (Sanborn, F.B., "The Social Sciences, Their Growth and Future," *The Journal of Social Science* XXI [1886]: 7-8).

Just as Francis Greenwood Peabody was concerned to introduce young persons to social problems and to prompt them to dedicate their talents to the alleviation of the conditions that created them, so a deep social passion has been a central factor in the odyssey of many who have subsequently taught Christian ethics. Certainly the experience of a ministry in Hell's Kitchen was pivotal in shaping the academic career of Walter Rauschenbusch, and the experience of pastoring auto workers in Detroit influenced Reinhold Niebuhr's teaching ministry in numerous ways. There are many members of the Society of Christian Ethics who first became interested in the study of Christian ethics from a passion, however modest, to do something about social evils. The decision to teach social ethics was their attempt to give pedagogical shape to such deep underlying concerns, and this often brought them into teaching situations having a professed identification with Christian faith. Dombrowski points out that in the concluding two decades of the last century those with social concerns frequently ended up teaching in seminaries, and the same may be said for a number of those who have belonged to the Society in its first twenty-five years. However, one of the important developments that has taken place during the life of the Society has been the spread of the field into colleges and universities. That change in the location where many members of the Society did their teaching took place at the time when neutralism was becoming increasingly prevalent in the academic world, and when excellence in the mastery of a discipline was becoming more respected than the impulse for social reform. Partly because of this, the formation of The American Society of Christian Social Ethics (as it was first named) came about from quite different impulses that did the initial teaching of Christian social ethics.

The reasons for the founding of the Society were partly logistical and stemmed from the desire of those already teaching Christian social ethics in the late 1950's to have greater interchange with each other. The Society was formed because these persons sought a professional identity separate from the professors of such subjects in the seminary curriculum as religious education, homiletics, and worship. The Society's formation is probably best understood as a part of what Christopher Jencks and David Riesman have identified as the academic revolution, which placed more and more emphasis in higher education on disciplinary self--awareness. The academic revolution located the teacher in the connectionalism of a discipline more than in the camaraderie of a cause or in the community of a single institution. It was buoyed by an expansion of colleges and universities to meet postwar needs. That considerable growth in the size of institutions was accompanied by the introduction, often for the first time, of the teaching of religious studies, even in colleges and universities having no confessional or ecclesial identity. The increase of people teaching religion in the broader humanistic sense had a component in the increase in those teaching Christian social ethics, although the growth of the Society of Christian Ethics has been relatively modest in comparison with the growth over the corresponding period of the group known in the 1950's as the National Association of Biblical Instructors and more recently as the American Academy of Religion.

The development of the Society was affected both by the growth in the numbers teaching social ethics and related subjects and by the tendency of academics in those times to locate themselves among other academics teaching the same subject in other institutions. During much of the period covered by this study there has been a concern among some of its members to develop a still more careful delineation of Christian social ethics as a field. This concern owes a great deal of its inspiration to Walter G. Muelder, who has frequently pled for a genuinely interdisciplinary field in which the "practitioners undertake joint theoretical and empirical studies in theology, ethics, and the behavioral and historical sciences." ("Christian Social Ethics Bookshelf," *The Christian Century* 30 [October 30, 1963]: 1336.) In 1972 Paul Deats, Jr., one of Muelder's close associates, observed that clarity in methodology was long in coming and suggested that ". . . social ethics must become more systematic and rigorous in clarifying definitions, employing more adequate concepts, and testing generalizations and theoretical probes." ("The Quest for a Social Ethic," Paul Deats, Jr., ed., *Toward a Discipline of Social Ethics* [Boston University Press, 1972]: 72). Elaborating on this point, Deats indicated what would be entailed in developing a more self-conscious understanding of social ethics as a discipline:

> The movement toward such a discipline would seem to involve at least the following: (1) a self-conscious community of inquiry and exchange, with a continuing attempt to focus on commonly defined problems; (2) an interdisciplinary effort to work out the understanding of what constitutes an ethical issue in social policy; (3) an evolving body of knowledge, with principles of evaluation; and (4) a reflective alternation between detachment--with attention to theory--and involvement--with concern for practice. *(Ibid., 42).*

The life of the Society has provided something quite close to the first of the conditions identified by Deats as necessary for the emergence of a discipline, though not, perhaps, with as clear a view of the problems to be faced as might be called for. It has made some contribution to the second of the conditions, though there have been only a few representatives of such particular disciplines as philosophy, sociology, and law among its members to make the mix truly interdisciplinary. The meetings of the Society and the publications flowing from those meetings have provided a large body of material with which to work, but less agreement as to how that material is to be evaluated. Finally, the Society has discussed the interaction between detachment and involvement, leaving its members to work out their own resolution of this tension with a touch of fear and trembling. These are contributions to the development of a discipline in the sense that Deats and Muelder have envisioned it, but hardly a finished product.

On balance, it must be admitted that there has been very little success over the years in achieving a theoretical consensus as to how Christian social ethics should go about its task, and probably little more consensus about the methodology of Christian ethics. Members of the Society often do their own thing, or things, in quite different ways. They are held together by common interests and personal loyalties as much or more than by a clear definition of a discipline as such. Perhaps this renders the field weak. Perhaps it undercuts its credibility among those who are especially self-conscious about academic matters. Perhaps it furnishes an unfinished agenda that should be pursued with greater zeal in the second quarter of the Society's life. Perhaps it suggests that the burden of social concern spills beyond the perimeters of the academic enterprise in the strictly disciplinary sense.

The Significance of the Names

One of the best ways to examine how the Society has understood itself over the years is to look at the various names it has adopted to describe itself. The frequent name changes--which may be a bit unique among professional groups--reveal the complexities involved in thinking about the field (or fields) of Christian ethics. Behind the changes it is possible to discover disagreements about, or at least shifts in, the way the membership has seen itself and its scholarly calling. Each of the words in the names of the Society has, over the years, been both a source of identity and a matter of friendly contention.

The first name change took place with the founding of the Society. The term "seminary professors," was prominent in the title of the parent or forerunner group, and was dropped from the designation given to the new organization. It came to be generally recognized, and rather commonly acknowledged, that scholarship in the field need not be carried on only in institutions that train the professional clergy despite some long historic ties between social ethics and seminary teaching. The Society has never assumed that Christian social concern is a clerical monopoly. But neither has it ever felt that scholarly integrity is somehow difficult to reconcile with the practice of ministry. In this latter respect life in the Society has been significantly different from that in much American higher education during the period. Schools of divinity in colleges and universities have not always had an easy time of it being accepted as full partners in the scholarly communities in which they have been located. Some divinity schools have even been dissolved or allowed to wither because the surrounding academic community has not regarded them as important or felt them to be worthy of significant support. This problem has not been present in the life of the Society, nor has there ever been a conscious separation between the clergy and lay members of the group. The shift away from a membership composed largely of those who teach in seminaries to a more composite group has not expressed itself as a repudiation of those at work in schools of divinity, but rather as a welcoming of those with similar interests working in more general educational settings, whether in college teaching, church related bureaucracies, or other kinds of professional activities. A common interest in the subject matter has held the Society together and enabled it to transcend differences that in many other settings have been matters occasioning open breaks or subtlely covert suspicions.

The scholarly self-identification of the Society has enabled it to bring together persons from many different branches of the Christian tradition. In particular, the Society was remarkably swift to facilitate collegiality between Protestants and Roman Catholics once the door to such cooperation was opened even to the slightest extent. The collegiality between these two groups quickly became as complete as the collegiality within either of them. This was no perfunctory ecumenism, but a true coming together on the basis of scholarly endeavour and mutual concern that has been one of the rich aspects of the Society's life. It has led, in several cases, to other interchanges as members of the Society have been invited to participate in many of each other's activities. Moreover, this collegiality has withstood some tensions that have arisen from the fact that there remain some fundamental differences about social policies (like abortion) between these two groups.

The Society's membership has also included some representatives of groups whose attitude on the nature of Christian social responsibility differs from that of most main line Christian practice. There are among its members some who belong to traditions that require an intentionally different life style of their members . For instance, some members of the Society come from groups that understand Christian discipleship to require a very clear separation from those political uses of power and entrepreneurial manipulations that are so much a part of military/industrial complexes and a technical/commercial world in general. Some members of the Society have similar convictions about the incompatibility of Christian discipleship and participation in the world of ordinary affairs, but are not identified with an intentional tradition. The proportion of those having such commitments may not be high, since by the very nature of their position those holding to such a view of Christian discipleship may not be regular joiners of main line bodies, but their presence has been an important witness among us. In contrast to those who stress Christian distancing from the world, there are members of the Society whose interpretation of Christian realism makes the use of power one of the main criteria of social responsibility--even some whose position in this regard veers toward an embrace of *realpolitik*. However vehement has been the polemic between these contrasting approaches outside, in the Society they have been respected by, and respectful of, each other.

In another contrast, not precisely congruent with the two attitudes just described, there are those who see the American experiment as having gone awry--having replaced its dedication to freedom and belief in equality for all people with an exercise of hegemonous power used mainly for the protection of economic privilege both at home and abroad. There are others who see the American dream, whatever its imperfections, as a remaining hope and symbol of freedom in a world of rampant collectivistic tyranny. These two groups are not unaware of the tensions between them--though those tensions have led to polemics that have been exchanged more sharply outside of the Society than within its gatherings. In the Society there has been a semblance of community maintained, and in many cases, even communication.

But there are limits to the inclusiveness which the Society has been able to achieve. In a paper, "Liturgy and Ethics," given at the January 1979 meeting and later published in *The Journal of Religious Ethics* VII, (Fall 1979): 162, Paul Ramsey suggested: "Our Society will not be truly national until Evangelicals are made welcome among us, brought into our dialogue, get on the program, etc." Of course there have been individual evangelicals in our midst, many of whom have made distinctive contributions both to the field and to the Society. But those particular evangelicals who have been most at home among us have been just as estranged as have been our other members from another kind of evangelical with high public visibility and a sizable conservative following. During the lifetime of the Society, indeed mainly in the latter few years of its history, groups of politically conservative and doctrinally fundamentalist Christians who once eschewed the idea of social Christianity have taken a new (and, to many, a disturbing kind of) interest in political issues. Many of them now champion an approach to public questions that is at odds with much that has been taken for granted within the confines of our group. This presents the Society with a challenge--made poignant by Ramsey's observation. Are we to assume that the ideological split between the kind of thinking in the Society (with all its contrasts) and the kind of thinking done by the resurgent right wing is so great that it is foolish to anticipate any dialogue with each other? Or, are we to hope and act on the belief that barriers can be surmounted--even in this area--by a combination of scholarly fairness and theologically rooted grace? Are we to treat the obvious appeal which such conservatism has to a large part of the public by dismissing it merely as a pandering to a desire for escape from worldly cares, or are we to see that such groups speak to many people who are deeply concerned about the losses of integrity and erosions of disciplined fidelity that have become too prevalent features of modern society?

The next name change took place in 1964, five years after the Society was founded. The adjective "social" was dropped from the title. It was argued that the adjective was redundant--that all ethics are by their very nature social in character. Properly understood, Christian ethics should involve social concerns, and Christian social ethics interfaces theological endeavors (such as moral theology and theological ethics) with disciplines such as law, sociology, anthropolgy, politics and economics. The change of name indicated that those with theological competence could be members even if they were not adept in the social scientific study of religion or versed in some other academic skills useful to an interdisciplinary approach. Those who thought of themselves more as sociologists than as theologians would be welcome if they were willing to converse across the interface. Frequently those who have considered themselves Christian sociologists have made the church or the professional practice of ministry their special concern. Some of them remained in the Society despite the subtle shift of focus that took place in its orientation. Such scholars might have been more comfortable with a name that explicitly embraced a more empirical approach to the study of religion and society rather than leaving to inference the understanding they were welcome and even necessary to the agenda of the group. It is probably correct to say that, on balance, the Society has come to attract those who identify more with a theological methodology than with a sociological one, that is, if either has to be taken by itself. This may be one of the reasons why, during the life of the Society of Christian Ethics, a number of its members have joined with scholars having more direct interests in sociological investigation in the activities of the Society for the Scientific Study of Religion, which does stress the empirical approach more consistently than does the SCE.

From different perspective the removal of the term "social" from the name of the Society either reflected or has helped to prompt another tendency in its life. The Society has been--as we have already noted--a professional, scholarly, association having Christian social action as an object of its study. It has also been, as we have noted, an academically oriented community that has accepted participation in confessional communities by its individual members as fully compatible with scholarly achievement. The Society has not, however, been a social action group--a fact that has sometimes been a source of concern for certain of its members. Dieter Hessel's paper, "Solidarity Ethics: A Public Focus for the Church," read at the 1977 meeting, raised questions about the life of the Society in this particular. Hessel noted that the tendency of Christian ethicists over the years has been to gravitate toward a professional academic posture, and he urged members of the Society to remember that the discipline began with an attention to the social question that was at least as much oriented to social reform as it was concerned with scholarly pursuits. He spoke of the value of a "*koinonia* of concern" that focuses on the struggle to meet social needs and that strives for social justice in the world. He mentioned as his model the Fellowship of Socialist Christians and might well also have suggested the Fellowship of Southern Churchmen.

Certainly it does not follow that keeping the word "social" in the name of the Society would have made a major qualitative difference in its life. The pressure for academic professionalism was in the very atmosphere at the time when the Society was discovering its identity. But the issue raised by the removal of the word does not go away. The history of the Action/Reflection Group shows that the concern that was articulated by Hessel has been shared by many for a long time within the life of the Society. That group tried to bring the reflective scholarly aspect of doing Christian ethics together with an active participatory aspect. Few members of the Society took issue with such premises, but a relatively small number of its members were ready to make the necessary change in professional posture that would have been entailed in making concerns about social questions a matter of group action rather than of group inquiry.

Hessel was pleading for a *praxis* within a confessional group seeking to be faithful to the Word in a hostile environment. He envisioned the need to struggle against deepening human privation, against social wrong-doing, and against economic self-interest. He was correct in observing that it has not been the history or the character of the Society to undertake that kind of struggle. He was also correct in observing that to a significant extent the Society had evolved a posture that was different from that which characterized much early teaching of Christian social ethics. Perhaps this primarily academic posture of the Society--which was shaped during the consolidation of the welfare state--will not be adequate for the future. The nation seems presently headed toward a democratically and publicly approved repudiation of the welfare vision, and toward the embrace of values that place more reliance upon the possession of power than upon the achievement of righteousness, that judges privilege more important to safeguard than equity, that considers entrepreneurial success more to be honored than compassion, and that often emphasizes the place of coercive discipline, police power, and military force in the preservation of order. Under these circumstances, many members of the Society may well feel the need for making something like a Barman declaration that says "No" to a national agenda that includes so many things that remind us of values cherished by fascism. The Society may find itself a group in which many members are prompted to examine the historical precedents and theological legitimations for a renewed concern about the social question. But are Barman declarations ever made by strictly academic groups--or only by confessing bodies? The academic vehicle, for all the values it does embody, and for all the collegiality it does make possible, may not have the spiritual resources to resist cultural and political malignancy. However, it can help those who come to feel the need of making a witness to find ways to make it boldly, and it may help them to do so with a greater understanding and wiser appreciation of its significance. Moreover, it is probably fair to suggest that the Society, despite its general tendency to be somewhat conservative, would be at least as likely to nurture the kind of understanding and witness that may be needed in a period of heightened societal injustice as would parish experience in most main line church bodies.

The discussions about the name change that took place in 1980 raised an entirely different set of issues. These issues are to be understood as much in light of what was not done as in what was done at the time of this, the last, tinkering with our designation. The decision to drop the term "American" had more symbolic than substantive import. (A proposal to replace the term "American" with "North American" generated some initial support but was defeated.) From the very first, membership and participation in the Society had been shared alike by persons in the United States and Canada. The decision to drop the term "American" took away whatever chauvinism might lurk in a title that could be read as referring only to the United States. However, when the Society dropped the term it did not, by this action, become any more international. The proportion of Canadian members did not change, nor did the orbit of the Society's influence suddenly expand. A little greater effort was started to make the members of the Society aware of the *Societas Ethicas*, our counterpart on the European continent with a membership of 233 in October of 1981. A copy of their membership roster was included in one of our mailings and our members were urged to make contact with their members as travels and scholarly endeavours made that possible. Very few of our members have availed themselves of that suggestion. Clearly, there is much more that can be done to facilitate interchange between these two kindred bodies, both by alerting our members to become more interested in the *Societas Ethicas* and in getting their members to be more interested in us. We might also do well to consider how to interest Latin American scholars in membership, and to bring more ethicists from overseas into some kind of association with us. If, as has been pointed out by Walbert Bulhmann in *The Coming of the Third Great Church* (Orbis Books, 1977) the majority of Christians will be living south of the equator within a decade, it will not prove satisfactory to have a Society that facilitates interaction only between persons living and working in North America or on continents bordering the North Atlantic.

Even more significant issues of purpose and identity were involved in the decision that was made in 1980, after much discussion, to keep the term "Christian ethics" rather than move to the phrase "religious ethics" for the name of the Society. In deciding to stay with the original designation the membership turned back at least two different impulses. There was, on the one hand, a feeling that the term "Christian" was a possible stumbling block to Jewish scholars who are concerned with many of the same issues as members of the Society. There were four Jewish scholars on our rolls in 1979 and it is not clear how many others would have joined a renamed group. Undoubtedly their contributions would be of enormous value, as the task force on the relationship between Jewish and Christian ethics made clear. The programs would undoubtedly have begun to take Jewish thinking more into account, for its own (and continuing) significance and not merely as background for (or comparison with) Christian reflection. Moreover, the Society would probably have felt it appropriate to shift its meeting time so as to avoid the Sabbath and thus make it possible for more Jewish scholars to be present.

Another impulse behind the proposal to designate the society with the term "religious ethics" was the feeling that the academic study of religion in colleges and universities had broken out of Christian confines. By changing its name the Society would take note of this and place itself squarely in the academic context of religious studies--eliminating any possible stigma that members of pluralistically oriented departments of religion would suffer from being identified with a group having a name that could be taken as indicating a confessional identity instead of a focus of inquiry. On a purely pragmatic level it might have made it easier for some members to claim travel funds to meetings in instances where the scholarly nature and functions of the Society were difficult to interpret to secular educators or to bursars with an eye on avoiding the use of public monies for specifically religious purposes.

The decision to retain the designation "Christian" rather than to move to the term "religious" should be understood in relationship to many of the things that have been observed about the nature of the Society in the discussion in the forepart of this chapter. Throughout the history of the Society, academic and professional considerations have proven more operative than social action concerns or confessional identities. In the decision it took respecting the last proposed name change, the Society drew back from the total embrace of prevailing academic tendencies to regard concern about just one tradition with something akin to suspicion. The decision, therefore, possibly represents a mood contrasting with, though by no means repudiating, the Society's tendency throughout much of its life to become more and more academic. It would no more be pushed wholly into a neutral or secular academic milieu than it would stay confined to a confessional one.

In addition to shying away from the complete embrace of the pluralistic/secular mind-set of the university, the Society was also saying that the Christian tradition is sufficiently large and broad in and by itself to demand the complete attention, or certainly to constitute the governing focus of inquiry, for this particular group. The membership as presently constituted could not presume to be skilled scholars of religious ethics in the broad sense. While some of its members, only a handful at that, were exploring comparative religious ethics as an ancillary interest, there were hardly enough of them working with sufficient thoroughness or breadth in those directions to transform the present group into a whole new entity. In sum, the Society was saying that, although it welcomes members from any (or even from no) religious tradition, it would keep its focus on how one tradition thinks and acts, or upon how that tradition can be understood from the perspective of other traditions, rather than on how all traditions are equally understood.

The Dynamics of Bonding

Although the major impulses for the founding of the Society of Christian Ethics were logistical and professional, sharing in many respects the pedagogical professionalism of the academic revolution, the Society has never become simply and solely a professional organization in the narrow sense of that term. The programs of the meetings have not been dominated by persons mainly trying to increase their visibity or to buck for promotion. The Society has never operated a placement service and its meetings have seldom seen large numbers of people sneaking off to hotel rooms or other gathering places for interviews or other job hunting rituals. Moreover, the Society has not been a group of people talking about what is going on elsewhere, but a gathering of those who have been the makers of the discipline itself. It is difficult to identify any productive American scholar in the field of Christian ethics who has not participated in the life of the Society.

It is not easy to convey, without appearing to be triumphalistic, the sense of collegiality which is found--for many, in a unique way--in the life of the Society. Many of our members, active in a variety of professional academic groups and in social action movements of different kinds, report that life in the Society has a unique quality. As one of them put it, "SCE meetings are really old home week for most of us, sometimes the only place where one finds colleagues of very high caliber with the same passions and fascinations (and, I am sure, foibles) that preoccupy us most of our working days amidst colleagues with quite different agendas. The fabric and tissue of interaction outside the sessions and in late night discussions at these meetings is simply not present most places---it approximates Aristotle's Friendship."

Something powerful holds the Society together. It is nothing less than a bonding of informed concern--a bringing together of those whose scholarship has both an intrinsic value and a social reason for being. This may be a transmuted extension of the very same impulse that prompted Peabody, Rauschenbusch, and Niebuhr to be pioneers in our discipline. While the Society has never been the structural channel of direct social action, it has been a place from which to have the wellsprings of social caring refurbished with the living waters of substantive input and prophetic insight. Every prophet needs a quiet place of nourishment as well as a market place for proclamation, and every scholar who would take the social question or social questions seriously must have a place where insights are gathered, understandings compared, information acquired, and thought re-envisioned. Many have come to the meetings of the Society year-by-year precisely because they have felt these things to happen--perhaps in an unplanned way--at its gatherings. As measured on some scales, the Society has been conservative--surely its members do not all share an activist agenda or radical leanings. It has been concerned not to take action as much as to understand why action has to be taken, not to dictate agendas but to see why values have to be made socially functional, not to plump for a single point of view but to recognize why commitments are important to social well-being.

Another possible explanation for the success of the Society is its modest size. It has not grown unwieldy. It still has a sense of having a single corporate identity and not of being merely an umbrella for a host of diverse pursuits. The fact that it has kept to the practice of having a goodly number of plenary sessions at each annual meeting helps to insure that everyone has some experiences in common. Moreover, its members treat the business meetings with respect and participate with zest. The resultant decisions reflect the deliberative will of the group as a whole rather than the private agenda of a special cadre. Lastly, the membership has suffered little turn-over and many of those who were present "at the creation" still attend the meetings with remarkable regularity. Regionalism has not become widespread, and where it has developed it supports rather than competes with the activities and programs of the parent body.

Along with these grand commitments and ideal conditions the Society has been held together by dedicated leadership. The willingness of its members to be personally involved in its governance and supportive of its operations is a not inconsiderable source of its strength. The Society has never been managed by those making its operation their main calling and chief means of professional livelihood. Across the years it has spent but a fraction of its budgetary resources on administrative costs and services. Year after year the nominations committees have come up with candidates willing to give themselves voluntarily to the work of making policy and of performing all the many logistical operations that turn policy from mere resolve to living accomplishment.

The major work falls on the program committee that meets each spring to plan for the meeting the next January. That committee has been composed of the officers and some co-opted persons in the vicinity of its place of meeting. The editor of *The Annual* carries a particularly heavy responsibility. To collect the papers, coordinate the judgment of the paper selection committee, decide with the editorial board which ones to publish, gather other kinds of contributions, and see *The Annual* made camera-ready for publication, is a major set of tasks. Not all of those who give papers at the annual meetings are zealous about putting them into written form or seeing that they are submitted on time. The editor of *The Annual* has in recent years helped to see that papers are systematically collected and properly channeled into the archives of the Society. That obligation might well be made a regular part of the editor's task, especially if no one else is officially designated to be the ongoing archivist of the Society.

But all these important factors in explaining the coherence of the Society pale besides the significance of the work performed across the years by the executive secretaries. More than any other factor, the life of the Society has been sustained and nurtured by these persons who have the longest tenures of any officers and perform the most demanding duties. The executive secretaries have been most directly responsible for the ongoing activities of the organization, and have helped to maintain the Society's identity--its continuity between past, present, and future. The executive secretaries carry out decisions and policies made by the board, by the executive committee, by the members at the annual business meeting, and by the program committees. This requires them to perform myriad detailed tasks and to make independent decisions at various points. They assist the president and others in numerous ways, a process that requires sensitivity to yearly changes in leadership style and tact in the exercise of an office that must work with such changes.

One valuable function of the executive secretary is to reflect from time-to-time about the direction in which the Society is moving and the ways in which things are being done. The executive secretary must help other officers to think about the need for possible change. The executive secretary, who is the most visible person in the ongoing life of the Society, maintains contact with as many members as possible, knows their interests and contributions to the field, assists in processing the applications of new members and seeing that their names are placed on appropriate mailing lists, pays the bills and keeps financial records up-to-date, and maintains connections with the Council for the Study of Religion. Although the executive secretary may look busy at the annual meeting, the responsiblities carried at that time are only a fraction of the tasks which must be performed. Most of the work is done from week to week throughout the year through correspondence and frequent long distance telephone calls. As Joseph Allen approached the end of his term of service he drew up a list of the duties involved. That list is seven pages long--single spaced! It indicates what a continuous and complex set of responsibilities has evolved upon the office of the executive secretary.

Some Conjectures About the Future

It is hazardous to look too far into the future, yet one cannot totally ignore the questions that seem likely to confront us as we move into the second quarter century of the Society's life. One of the most persistent questions is whether the intimate collegiality of the Society's life, which so many of its members understandably cherish, can be indefinitely sustained. Even if the increase in the number of people teaching in the discipline has begun to taper off (which is by no means clear), the relatively rapid growth in the size of the Society in the last several years does make it necessary to ask whether it will be as possible to have a sense of scholarly bonding among six or seven hundred as it has been to have it among one, or two, or three hundred members. Moreover, the next decade will see many who have been members of the Society from its very founding retire from active teaching, shy away from winter-time travel, and find themselves unable to continue the kind of participation that has provided a special continuity during so much a part of the past twenty-five years of the Society's life.

Moreover, the cost of holding national meetings has greatly increased in recent years, and a wholly different pricing pattern for air travel has come into effect. Unless institutional budgets escalate, it will be increasingly difficult to gather a large proportion of the members in a single meeting. The pressure to make regional groups more active--with all the changes that pattern could bring about--may well increase irresistibly.

Another question that may confront us is whether we are being faithful if we talk mainly to ourselves. When one considers how small the membership of the Society is in comparison with the whole academic enterprise, or the population of the country as a whole, it does make it necessary to ask how large a group has to be in order to have a significant public influence. Perhaps it is not size but posture that counts. There is great value in talking to one another, which is possible in such a small group--that we should cherish and continue to do so. But if talking to each other means we talk <u>only</u> to ourselves, then we shall have betrayed the impulses that gave birth to Christian social ethics a hundred, and to the Society itself twenty-five years ago.

We run the danger of talking only to ourselves in several ways. One way is to be interested only in the professional group itself, run around only with our own kind, pay attention only to those who pursue the same kind of teaching and academic research as we pursue, or reassemble the very same set of people in other organizations to which we belong. That is a heady and exciting kind of life to live, but does it suffice even as a scholarly service? Another way of talking only to ourselves is to write professional papers only for this group, or for the very same colleagues assembled in other groups, and not to prepare materials which the general citizenry or membership of the churches can read. Is it enough for the study of Christian ethics to be a self-sustaining enterprise done mainly for its own sake and the innate satisfactions it yields, and not for the sake of some large public good? The greatest question for the future may well be, not whether Christian ethics as a discipline remains a viable concern of a handful of scholarly types, but whether Christian commitment finds and maintains a significant place among a broader constituency, both in the North American orbit and in other vital parts of a shrinking globe.

Christian ethics will be likely to be robust in the future only if there are vibrant communities of Christian faith all over the world and viable Christian institutions in the places where Christian ethicists try to work. It is by no means sure that Christian faith will remain particularly vital in the places it has flourished in the past. Culture faith and "main street" religiosity are too pervasive in their consequences merely to be ignored or simply by-passed in a more specialized attention to the niceties of academic pursuits, and, if they wholly conquer institutional Christianity in the North American scene, the impact upon the academic enterprise of Christian ethics as it has been practiced in the Society will be debilitating. Then too, there are many parts of the church that regard the scholarly and the academic enterprise with distrust, if not with disdain. If the institutional expressions of Christianity as we know them in our immediate milieu progressively decline in quality, even if they do survive, that also will undermine the possibility of doing Christian ethics well. Unless we address these deteriorating conditions in both church and culture and find ways to cope with them, the commitment of the Society to the learned study of a Christian response to social questions may come to very little. If robust Christian ethics can exist only within a context of vibrant faith and viable Christian institutions, and if those very contexts are eroding right under our very noses, then business as usual for a Society such as ours will not insure a promising future.

In his provocative and suggestive treatment of theological education, Edward Farley talks about the trends toward specialization that have made each of the branches of theological study something of an academic speciality rather than an expression of a more unifying theological enterprise. "Each [of the disciplines]," he writes, "gathered the sociological accoutrements of a science: the research-oriented journals, the professional society, the graduate program in that science alone, the delimitation of research projects within the bounds (the language, methods, literature) of that science, the nationwide or worldwide collegium of scholars in that science." (Edward Farley, *Theologia: The Fragmentation and Unity of Theological Education*, (Fortress Press, 1983.) There is a sense in which that has happened within the field of Christian ethics though perhaps not quite to the same extent or with the self-conscious intensity that it has happened to some other academic disciplines. Farley then suggests ways in which the theological school should move to a more inclusive whole, for which he employs the old term *Theologia*--a term which implies a conjuction of the active and contemplative life.

We will no more be helped to bring reflection and practice into a closer conjunction by what has occurred in higher education in general in recent years than by what has happened in much ecclesiastical life. While in the case of the theological enterprise ministerial practice has too frequently become an highly individualized caring for personal needs apart from any social transformation, in the case of higher education, a narrow professionalism has appeared that treats employability as the bottom line. Christian social responsibility cannot be significantly advanced by either.

The Society of Christian Ethics is a young organism--vigorous, healthy, enthusiastic. It has come through its birth, weaning, growth, and major period of skill development with remarkable success. It is, hopefully, ready to contribute rather than merely to take sustenance from its social world, to enter the serving task of inquiry and public responsibility. Perhaps the greatest contribution it can render in this regard, without repudiating the main thrust of its early life, is to ask how it can move toward the kind of total undertaking which Farley has in mind, or to the kind of great concern about the condition of society itself that ought to be the central reason for either the university or the seminary to exist.

The same year in which Peabody began teaching social ethics at Harvard, the report of the American Social Science Association, which became the professional association of the then embryonic field of sociology, contained these words of its secretary, Professor F. B. Sanborn of Cornell University: ". . . for we cannot too often consider and repeat that the origin of every science and preeminently of the social sciences is divine." That perspective hardly thrives in the university today, nor are the social sciences much more adept at fostering social concern than other branches of learning. The Society of Christian Ethics has shared the impulses that have brought the intellectual disciplines to a new perspective on themselves and the world, but perhaps it has another calling to pioneer--one that will involve questioning whether these discipline-oriented developments in the academic enterprise have made us sufficiently adequate to meet the challenges of circumstances in which the cry for justice cannot be indefinitely ignored with impunity and threats of ever increasing retribution cannot be relied upon interminably for ordering the world.

The growing human being may be said to take more away from its environment during the first twenty-five years of its life than it contributes. But unless that pattern reverses, and during the subsequent twenty-five or so years the human being contributes more than it takes away from its surrounding communities, then we say that the human being has not reached full maturity. At twenty-five years of age the time of introspective and self-oriented development should be over. The time for increased responsibility has begun. If we can say at this juncture that the Society has grown up and is strong and vibrant, may it be possible to say in another twenty-five years that the Society has matured and learned to play a prophetic and mediating role in helping Christians and their institutions, as well as the wider society, to join in moving toward a more just and compassionate ethos. The story of the next twenty-five years ought to trace the contributions of this group to the surrounding world with as much record of achievement as this account has traced the story of the birth, growth, and consolidation of the organization as an academic guild of remarkable quality.